# THE PORTLAND [MAINE] TRANSCRIPT

## 1869-1870

### News and Summary
### Marriages and Deaths

Compiled by
Elaine Morrison Fitch

HERITAGE BOOKS
2006

# HERITAGE BOOKS
*AN IMPRINT OF HERITAGE BOOKS, INC.*

**Books, CDs, and more—Worldwide**

For our listing of thousands of titles see our website
at
www.HeritageBooks.com

Published 2006 by
HERITAGE BOOKS, INC.
Publishing Division
65 East Main Street
Westminster, Maryland 21157-5026

Copyright © 2005 Elaine Morrison Fitch

Other books by the author:
New Hampshire Patriot and State Gazette *1835*
*Deaths, Marriages and Miscellaneous*
*Newspaper Abstracts from the Philadelphia Repository, 1803*
Portland Advertiser and Gazette of Maine*: Marriages, Deaths and News from November 1838-May 1839*
The 1848 Boston Cultivator*: Marriages, Deaths and Miscellaneous Readings*
The Boston Recorder and Telegraph, *1825*

All rights reserved. No part of this book may be reproduced or transmitted in any form or by any means, electronic or mechanical, including photocopying, recording or by any information storage and retrieval system without written permission from the author, except for the inclusion of brief quotations in a review.

International Standard Book Number: 978-0-7884-3272-9

Dedicated to

Patrick "Henry" Morrison

Ethel Mary Small Morrison

Other Books by Elaine Fitch:

*The 1848 Boston Cultivator:
Marriages, Deaths and Miscellaneous Readings*

*The Boston Recorder and Telegraph, 1825*

*Portland Advertiser and Gazette of Maine:
Marriages, Deaths and News, From November 1838 - May 1839*

*Newspaper Abstracts from the Philadelphia Repository, 1803*

*Independent Chronicle & Boston Patriot, 1839:
News Summary and Marine Disasters, Marriages and Deaths*

PORTLAND TRANSCRIPT

April 3, 1869

A writer in the Rockland Free Press who recently visited the State Prison, says;
I heard of a touching incident which occurred recently at the prison. Two ladies came, wishing to be shown through, and as they stepped into the wheel wright shop, the younger lady exclaimed "There he is! and," wept uncontrollably; the eyes of every prisoner but one were turned upon her, and that one kept his head down. The ladies exclaimed that they had a brother in the army from whom they never heard after a certain battle, in which they supposed he was killed. After a long time they heard something which convinced them that he was in prison, and for six months they had been traveling, and searching from him. The young lady said she met his eyes the instant the stepped into the shop, and the recognition was mutual.

The Gardiner Journal says that a young man named G. W. P. Ayer, son of J. B. Ayer, of New York, has been drawing checks on his father to a liberal extent, and they not being honored he has left for parts unknown.

Brother Shaw, of the Oxford Democrat, objects to having the low liquor store over his head for fear it will spill through and spoil a good editorial. It had better be over his head than under his nose.

The Maine Farmer says that he has good authority for saying that Gov. Chamberlain had no veto of the State Police bill prepared, and no assurance was given that the bill would be vetoed.

Mrs. Sarah Slater, the mother of the first child born in Washington, Me., died recently at the age of 89. The child is still living, at the age of 69.

The dwelling house of William Anderson, in Baileyville, with all its contents, was totally destroyed by the fire on the 18th ult. Loss about $1500.

Mr. Hiram H. Winslow, of Bethel, writes up that he has a silver coin which he plowed up on the intervale of the Androscoggin, where the Indians had camped in the early settlement of the town. It bears the date 1733, and from the description we take it to be a Spanish real of the reign of Philip V.

The dwelling house of Mr. Charles Austin in Windham, was so rapidly destroyed by fire on the 19th ult., that Mr. Austin, who lay sick in bed, was with great difficulty taken out of the flames. Nothing was saved except a little clothing. No insurance.

Thomas Cook, of Norridgewock, was instantly killed by the caving in of a large quantity of earth while at work on the Somerset Railroad one day last week. Another man was seriously, if not fatally injured.

At the present term of the Supreme Court at Augusta, Mrs. Serena Shaw of Waterville, recovered $1641.00 against Dr. Charles H. Rowell of Kendall's Mills for malpractice in reducing a dislocated leg.

A fire in Castine Saturday destroyed the store of McClusky and Co., tailors; Perkins & Co., grocers; Mr. Clark, books and shoes, and the dwelling house of Capt. Hodson, occupied by Capt. Pike.

The following postmasters have been appointed in Maine: Stephen C. Higgins, at the newly established office at North Milford; and Isaiah Chick at Madrid, Henry M. Bearce at Norway.

The match factory of Mr. Wilson Marston was destroyed by fire in Waterville, on Tuesday week, together with two drying houses and a stock of lumber. No insurance.

In Lewiston a girl named Joanna Hallisey returned from her work in the mill one evening recently ate her supper and rising therefrom fell dead. She was 17 years old.

The late Rev. Dr. S. L. Pomeroy was buried in his own family lot at Bangor, by the people to whom in early manhood he had ministered for twenty-three years.

Hon. F. A. Pike, and his wife, whose health is very poor, intend to take a trip to Europe, where they will spend the summer in the hope of restoring it.

Eastport is troubled with burglars.

The dwelling house of Rev. Aaron Clark, of Washington, was entirely destroyed by fire, with all its contents on the 18th ult. No insurance.

The dwelling house of James Miller, in Rockland, was burned with all its contents on Sunday morning. Loss $700; insured for $400.

Hon. T. S. Lang will sell his celebrated horses, colts, and neat stock, by auction at North Vassalboro, on the 11th of May. Prox.

Pierce Soule, once Senator of Louisiana, has become insane.

It is said the Ex-President Johnson left Washington with about $77,000

Ex-Mayor Harper, of New York was killed, last week, by being thrown from a carriage.

Brig Model, from Portland for Savannah, with a cargo of hay, was totally lost, last week; crew taken off and carried into Wilmington, N. C. She was owned in Eastport and was commanded by Capt. Johnson.

At Montra, Shelby County, Ohio, last week, the wife of George Fowler, driven to desperation by his brutal abuse of her through many months, rose from her bed and struck her sleeping husband twenty blows with an axe, killing him instantly, and mutilating his body in a shocking manner.

Nearly every lunatic asylum in Germany has a patient who believes himself to be Abraham Lincoln.

That was a cool remark of the wife of Twitchell, condemned for murdering his wife's mother: "By the way, when you see George, please ask him where he would like to be buried after his is hanged."

Mr. J. R. Milliken, the engrossing clerk in the Secretary of State's office, at Augusta , has been very ill ever since the adjournment of the Legislature, having been obliged at the close of the term to remain at his desk several nights until near morning–an over exertion which resulted in paralysis of the lower limbs.

## PORTLAND TRANSCRIPT

April 10, 1869
LETTER FROM BOSTON.
April 1st, 1869

Julia Ward Howe, last Sabbath, gave at the Horticultural Hall, a second discourse on religion in America. Her gifted mind has won her an enviable position in the literary world, and these recent essays are redolent with much of the spirit of truth as well as the breath of poetry. Although her liberalism may come short of what is regarded as "evangelical Christianity," it is far in advance of the views of many whom she addressed. Indeed she assailed the postulates, and overthrew the reasoning of a notorious "free thinker," who had preceded her. She showed that his depreciation of Christianity was unjust, if merely viewed in the light of history. Her vindication of the Puritans was admirably pronounced.

"What historic set of men have wrought better than they did? One would think that a prophetic insight had led them so to crowd their lives with zeal and labor, that they knew how brief was to be their period of ethical elaboration, how mighty the test to which it results would be brought. Accordingly they wrought with their might. Their music was a battle song, their Sabbath a labor of their soul. The noble fabric of the Puritans has stood, founded on a rock, and the gates of hell have not prevailed against it."

Mrs. Howe, evidently is not ready to follow the lead of F. E. Abbott, who writes, "Free religion has no church to maintain no rites of worship to perform, no Bible to believe, no Christ to obey." In burning words she replies, "if Christ was removed our institutions would shrink and darken. To take Christianity out of New England would be even more fatal than it would have been to have left New England out of the Union." Alluding to the fact that the day was Easter Sabbath, she gives this graceful peroration: "I bring in my basket only the fragments of the Divine feast from which I have again and again been refreshed and nurtured. Let your sympathy and kind interpretation renew a medieval miracle, and change my fragments into the garland of Easter roses which I would have woven for you, and which you and I would gladly hang before the niches that enshrines our dearest memories, our greatest blessings, our furthest hope." E.P.T.

Mrs. Charlotte N. Tewksbury, widow of the late Dr. Jacob Tewksbury, and mother of Dr. Tewksbury, of this city, died suddenly at her home in Oxford, on Monday week, at the age of 78 years. She arose in her usual health, and when engaged in her morning devotions passed away without apparent struggle or pain. To a woman of her Christian character, such an end was not death, but translation.

The heavy fall of snow this winter has proven destructive to crazy old barns. The roofs of numbers have been crushed in by the weight. In Strong, the other day, while Mr. Elisha G. Jones and his hired man, were at work in a shed, the roof yielded to the pressure of the snow, and they were buried beneath the fallen timbers and snow. They were dug out alive, but badly injured.

A neighbor going to the door of Mr. Richard Gage, at Woodford's Corner, Westbrook on Tuesday week, found Mrs. Gage alone in the house, in a dying state. When he returned with assistance she had expired. Mr. Gage had gone into the city for a nurse. The coroner's jury found that she came to her death by heart disease.

Miss Martha Holmes, of Freeport, in a temporary fit of insanity, jumped out of a window barefoot and in her night clothes, and lay on the cold snow two hours before she was discovered. She was just alive when found, and it was feared she had received so severe a shock that she could not recover.

Mr. John W. Pope, of Brewer, was seriously injured recently by falling from a ladder, a distance of fifteen feet, and striking on a stone doorstep. His side was badly injured and it is feared that his skull is slightly fractured.

The store of Mr. Friend, in Etna, was robbed of $1000 worth of dry goods on Friday week. The proprietor offered a reward of $150 for the detection of the thieves or recovery of the property.

The Dexter Gazette says that Mr. Oliver Lane, of that town, lost two valuable cows recently, and on examination it was found that their livers were almost completely wasted away.

Biddeford is infested with incendiaries. On Thursday night they burned the livery stable of G. L. Foss and the barn of George Scott, besides setting other fires.

Perry has elected a lady on the School Committee.

Col. E. W. Woodman, formerly commander of the Second Maine Cavalry, died in Madison County, Miss., on the 15th ult.

Mrs. Jane A. Howard, wife of Charles Howard, of Brooksville, on the 18th ult, presented her husband with three children at birth-two girls and a boy.

Who killed the State Police Bill? Hon. John L. Stevens denies that he did it, and Hon. J. G. Blaine denies that the Maine delegation in Congress urged its defeat. Mr. Nye says Hon. T. S. Lang told him they did. Mr. Lang says it is all a mistake; the bill the Congressmen objected to was that providing for biennial sessions and elections.

In Gorham, 26th ult., a little Indian girl named Capeon, nine years old, was caught in the belting of the main wheel of a bedstead factory, and carried over and over for fifteen minutes. When at last the mill was shut down the poor thing was dead and badly mangled, both feet being torn from her limbs and gathered up by themselves.

In Bath, on Friday week, the store of E. C. Sweet, occupied by William Greenleaf as a grocery, was destroyed by fire. The stock was nearly a total loss, with no insurance. The building was not insured.

Mr. B. F. Fowle, of Lewiston, baggage master on the Androscoggin, railroad, dislocated one of his shoulders on Saturday, by falling into the pit of the turn-table at Brunswick.

Rev. James B. Crawford, for many years principal of the East Maine Conference Seminary, died at his residence in Buckport at 10 o'clock on Wednesday evening.

Franklin J. Rollins, Esq., succeeds Hon. N. J. Miller as collector of Internal Revenue for this district. This is one of the rare cases of promotion for merit.

Paris has lost its oldest inhabitant, Mr. Ebenezer Tuell, who recently died at the age of 90 years, having spent 65 years upon the same farm.

Camden has been visited by incendiary fires, destroying a boat house and William Frye's fish house, involving a loss of $2000; partially insured.

The house of Mr. William M. Perkins, at West Poland, was recently very badly damaged by fire. He estimates his loss at more than $1000.

The barn and other property of J. Stevens, at East Windham, were destroyed by fire on the 26th ult., to the value of $2000. No insurance.

A son of Eben Littlefield, of Brooks, aged 15, had his leg badly broken above the knee, from a stone thrown from a blast on the railroad.

A little son of Claudia Favor, of Norway, aged four and a half years, was drowned on Monday week, while out at play with his sled.

Mr. Gorham G. Blake, of Belfast, fell overboard from a steamer on the Sacramento River, on the night of Feb. 24th., and was drowned.

Col. Lang, of Vassalboro, at his great sale of stock on the 11th May, will not dispose of the famous stallion, General Knox.

Queer things happen in New York. A dead body was found in the river with a dirk in its heart. Everybody said it was Count Wesser, an Austrian murdered by a husband whose wife he had seduced. But suddenly the Count appears alive and well, and going to see the murdered man, is so struck with the resemblance of the features to his own, that he exclaims in trembling accents, "Mine Got! dat ish not me!," as if to assure himself and his companions of his own existence. The affair is more mystery than ever.

The colored Lieutenant Governor of Louisiana was recently expelled from an omnibus in Louisville on account of his color, his fellow white passengers threatening to throw him out the window. The same gentleman a few days later, was cordially welcomed by Gen. Grant, with whom he had a private interview.

Horace Greeley's old white coat is almost of age; he bought it in London over twenty years ago.

Bishop Simpson says nobody can live at peace in Texas who doesn't denounce the government, abuse the Freedmen's Bureau, and curse the Negro.

Jenny Lind's daughter, twelve years old, exhibits much of her mother's great genius as a singer.

John R. King, of Mason County, Kentucky was recently killed by his son because he would not divide his estate with him.

A woman died in Virginia, the other day, at the age of one hundred and twenty-five years. She had Indian blood in her veins and must have been a member of one of the *"first families."*

Attorney General Hoar decides that the eight hour law cuts down the pay as well as the hours of labor. Mechanics in the Kittery Navy Yard remonstrate against the construction of the law.

Mrs. John Jacob Astor celebrated the coming of age of her son, by furnishing the money to provide one hundred orphan boys with homes in the west. This is better than spending $5000 on a birthday ball.

Pope Pius IX, in a letter, invites all "Christian mothers and daughters of Mary" to form a league against the doing up of *chignons,* and the arranging of tresses several times a day, which occupies the time that should be devoted to religious duties, pious works and family affairs.

Mr. James Collins, of Great Falls, N. H., who was bitten by a rabid dog two years ago, and experienced no trouble from the wound at the time was last week seized with hydrophobia, and became furious, severely biting a neighbor who was called in to assist in taking care of him. It was feared the case would result fatally.

The late James Harper sat for his photograph, and renewed his accidental life insurance policy, on the morning of the day of the accident which caused his death.

Everybody is puzzled how to account for Senator Sprague's late extraordinary speeches, especially since the Senator declares that he was neither drunk nor crazy.

In Montana they call marrying a squaw a "copper wedding.

Minnesota does not ally any of the school fund to go to schools from which colored children are excluded.

Africa is ahead of us in some respects. Consul Amos Perry says that female advocates are found in Tunis, whose distinct office is to manage the cases of women plaintiffs and defendants coming before the highest tribunal in the land.

Another startling development is made in the Hill murder at Philadelphia. It will be remembered that Mrs. Hill was murdered and thrown out of the window, and that her son-in-law, Twitchell and her daughter, were tried and the former found guilty, while the latter was discharged. The conduct of Mrs. Twitchell has recently excited suspicion, and Twitchell has now made a confession to the effect that his wife, unknown to him, killed her mother, and that he then helped her to throw the body out of the window and promised his wife not to reveal her crime. He now makes this disclosure that he may have peace with God. It is said the murderess left the city in anticipation of her husband's confession. The Philadelphia papers condemn the confession of Twitchell as a falsehood, and express a belief in the entire innocence of Mrs. Twitchell. On the other hand, those who knew her in Washington say her mother was the keeper of a house of questionable reputation, that Mrs. Twitchell was the illegitimate daughter of an Ohio member of Congress, and that she is the very woman to kill her mother, or commit any other crime that would benefit herself.

## MARRIAGES
In this city, April 5, by Rev. O. T. Moulton, Mr. Merrill P. Jordan, and Miss Emily E. Deering, daughter of Rufus Deering, Esq., all of Portland.
In Harrison, March 27, By Ezaa E. Ingalls, Esq., Mr. Alphonso Moulton and Miss Etta A. Ross, both of Harrison.

In Sedgwick, March 24, by Rev. Mr. Bartlett, Capt. H. R. Sargent, of Portland, and Eleanor W., daughter of Hon. William H. Sargent, of Sedgwick.

In North Yarmouth, by Rev. George A. Putnam, James Lawrence of Boston, and Miss Nellie M. Marston, of North Yarmouth.

In St. Andrews, N. B., on the 3rd ult., by Rev. W. Q. Ketchum, Mr. Henry F. Todd to Miss Mary R. McDonall, both of St. Stephen, N. B. no cards.

In Auburn, March 27th, Charles M. Brooks of Auburn, and Mary A. Annis, of Webster.

In Bath, March 29 Thomas McKay and Miss Mary A. Anderson.

In Lisbon, March 28, Mr. Isaac N. Beal, of Durham, and Miss Mary A. Sutherland, of Lisbon.

## DEATHS

In this city, March 31, Mr. Joseph Hale, aged 53.

In this city, March 31, Woodbury R., infant child of C. and A, M. Payson.

In this city, April 1, Ida J., daughter of A. J. and Sarah F. Soule, aged 1 year and 10 months.

In this city, April 1, Fred L. Boyd, aged 22 years.

In this city, March 30, Mr. John Morrison, formerly of Wells, aged 70 years, 4 months and 14 days.

In Saccarappa, March 15, James L. Mayberry, aged 22 years and 2 months.

In Lewiston, Marcy 27, William H. Bucknam, only child of Amos and Lydia Bucknam, aged 7 years and 5 months.

In Alfred, March 31, Georgie Carroll, youngest child of George H. and Marietta C. Webber, of Portland, aged 4 months and 22 days.

In Bath, April 1, Mr. Alexander Waterhouse, formerly of Portland, aged 74 years.

In Cape Elizabeth, March 30, Mrs. Sarah Cushing, aged 55 years and 11 months.

In Standish, March 31, Harriet M. wife of Horatio J. Swasey, aged 54 years.

In Brunswick, March 27, Mr. Micajah Haskell, formerly of Harpswell, aged 73 years.

In Vergens, Vt., March 30, Mrs. Susie Cummings, wife of W. S. Holland, of Vermont, and daughter of Leonard F., and Hannah S. Cummings, of Gray, aged 24 years.

In Limerick, March 10, of typhoid fever, Miss Mary Lizzie, only child of James and Sarah A. Perkins, aged 19 years and 11 months.

Thus in the spring time of life has been snatched away one of earth's sweetest flowers, the memory of whose dutiful affection and loving smile will ever abide with the heart-stricken parents as the sunshine of their lives. Though they feel that the light of their dwelling has been removed they know that it is not extinguished, but shines forth in all the souls' heaven born effulgence beneath the smile of the Father, and before whose throne they feel assured their Lizzie as singing with the angels and music such as only the blessed know now fills her soul with rapture.

Although a kind friend to all, yet especially to we, whose privilege it has been from time to time and from day to day to associate with her, feel that

"To know her well
Prolonged exalted bound enchantment's spell."
Many tender memories cluster around each heart which recall.
"A touch of the vanished hand
And a sound of the voice that is still."
And although
"This eye must be dark that so long has been dim,
Ere again it may gaze upon thine,
Yet my heart has revealings of them and home.
In many a token and sign:
I know thou art gone where thy forehead is starred.
With the beauty that dwelt in the soul.
Where the light of they loveliness cannot be marred,
Nor the heart be flung back from its goal.

"In thy far away dwelling where'er it may be,
I know thou hast vision of mine,
Thy love that made all things like music to me,
I have not yet learned to resign;
I never look up with a vow to the sky,
But a light like they beauty is there;
And I hear a low murmur like thine in reply
When I pour out my spirit in prayer."
H..E.P.

At Peaks Island, Portland Herald, March 13, Mrs. Philena, wife of Johiah Sterling, aged 62 years and 9 days.
For still her feature wore that light,
Which flits not with the breath,
And life ne'er looked more purely bright
Than in the smile of death.

# PORTLAND TRANSCRIPT

## April 17, 1869

On Wednesday week a locomotive on the grand truck exploded at Danville Junction, blowing the engine to atoms, tearing up the track, and breaking the glass in the passenger depot. A portion of boiler weighing nearly half a ton shot into the air, cut off a piece of a flag staff at an elevation of about eighty feet, and landed in a pasture nearly an eighth of a mile distant. The fireman Peter Doyle, of this city, was blown several yards into the air, and landed against a pile of wood ninety feet off. He was badly scalded and his ankle bone was splintered. Capt. Nathan Walker, of East Poland, Mr. George Cummings, of St. Johnsbury , Vt., Charles Robinson, a citizen of the place, and Capt. Hamilton, of Lewiston, received injuries more or less severe, but none of them fatal.

In Lewiston, some Irish boys were firing minnie balls across the river, when one of them entered a workshop and cut a big hole in the leather apron worn by Mr. T. J. Dawes, which fortunately was tough enough to arrest the ball. Mr. Dawes was stunned and bruised. The boys escaped.

The Farmington Chronicle say the Golden Wedding of Moses and Edna French, of Chesterville, was celebrated by their relatives and friends on the 25th ult., in an impromptu and very pleasant manner.

The father of Mr. M. Woodman of Farmington Falls, 77 years old, while at work in his son's factory on Saturday week, had all the fingers cut off one of his hands by coming in contact with a circular saw.

The explosion of a kerosene lamp in the dry goods store of Rev. W. Wyman, of Farmington Falls, on Saturday week, damaged goods to the amount of more that $1000.

On Wednesday week, Mr. Pollister, of New Gloucseter, brake–man on the grand trunk, was badly crushed while shackling carts at the Gilead station. His injuries were considered very serious.

Capt. Joshua F. Strout, of Cape Elizabeth had been appointed keeper of the Portland Light House in place of Mr. Elder Jordan, resigned.

Mr. Freeman Williams, of South Gardiner, chopped off one of his fingers from his left hand while cutting wood, one day last week.

On Thursday week, the dwelling of Mr. Reuben Howard at Rockville, was damaged by fire to the amount of $155.

The Ellsworth American says a number of men directed by a spiritualistic medium have been for some time engaged in making an excavation at Durgins Cave in Mt. Desest, after the hidden treasures of Capt. Kidd &c., which have so long disturbed the dreams of the money diggers, but no yellow or moon colored deposits have yet been found.

Arthur, son of Milton Gibson, of Kendall's Mill, while out gunning, on Wednesday week, was shot through the hand and arm, by the premature discharge of his gun. The ball lodged in his shoulder, tearing the flesh shocking, but there were hopes of his saving the arm.

In Belfast, Wednesday week, while Alex McDonald, a Nova Scotian, was engaged on the railroad works, in drawing a charge, it exploded, driving the tamping iron into his forehead, making a hole so that the brain ran out. He died the next morning.

The exhibition of the two upper classes at Bowdoin occurred on Monday week. Among the students who are reported to have acquitted themselves well are E. P. Payson of Westbrook, and Frank W. Ring and Willard Perley of Portland.

The match factory of B. Bunker & Co., Kendall's Mills, splits into "lucifers," nearly 1000 cords of pine wood, making 150,000 gross of matches. They also make five million flour barrel plugs a year for the western market.

The First Baptist Church, of Houlton, have been presented, by Jeremiah Curtis, of New York, with a church bell weighing half a ton, and it has been raised to its place in the tower of the new church.

Mrs. Mary, wife of Joseph F. Libby, of Dexter, was found on the 3rd inst., lying dead with her face in a little stream of water, four inches deep, near her house, She was about 64 years.

Mrs. Caroline Brown, mother of Artemus Ward, had the misfortune to slip on the ice a few days ago, and break her arm, at her residence at Waterford, says the Lewiston Journal.

An attempt was made on Wednesday night to fire the carriage house of Mr. Small, cashier of the National Bank, in Biddeford. A valuable rockaway was destroyed.

Mr. James Cary, of Bath, had his leg broken and severely crushed on Thursday week by a stick of timber striking it while he was at work in a ship yard.

Monday week, Mr. Charles Cutts of Kittery, an aged man was found dead in his bed. He had been insane for many years, and was in feeble health.

William P. Stetson, a son of "Father Stetson," had been appointed postmaster at Brunswick, in place of Mr. Crawford, who had become insane.

On Monday week, Mr. Withee, of South Dover Mill's while loading logs on a sled, fractured his leg, and was otherwise severely injured.

Ball & Smith's saw mill in Hollis, with about 500,000 feet of logs, was carried away by a recent freshet.

William County, while standing near the hatchway of one of the Biddeford mills, had two of his toes crushed by the falling of the elevator.

In Augusta, on Saturday week, a young man named Marston performed the foolhardy feat of sailing over the dam on a wager of $25. In the presence of a large group of spectators he shot over the edge of the dam in a small wherry with fearful celerity, disappeared in the boiling surge below, but instantly reappeared and rode safely out into the stream amid the cheers of the crowd. The height of the falls is thirty feet.

Mr. Waterhouse and his wife, of Bath recently died within little more than a week of each other, and a married daughter, who was with her mother, was taken violently insane the day before her death.

A lady named Gilkey of Augusta, was fatally injured Friday afternoon by falling down the cellar stairs. Her skull was fractured in two places and a portion of the brain protruded through the wound.

In Rockland, on Saturday, a storehouse filled with stoves, owned by Cobb, Wright & Norton, was destroyed by fire, together with a large blacksmith shop. Loss $2000; no insurance.

Robert Stuart, of Smyrna, fell dead in the road on Tuesday week. He was a stout and apparently healthy man, 38 years old. He leaves a wife and a large family of children.

Ex-secretary Stanton is dangerously ill.

A nephew of Sir Walter Scott died in Montreal, Thursday.

Miss Ida Lewis, the young heroine of Newport Harbor, has saved eight or nine persons from drowning. Citizens of Rhode Island propose to bestow upon her a life boat, and she has been presented with other gifts.

Pierre Soule is going to be sent to an insane asylum.

Senator Pomeroy, is going to address the Mormons in favor of female suffrage.

Among the ladies present at Mrs. Grant's reception, Tuesday week, were Mrs. John A. Peters and Mrs. John A. Poor, of this state.

Ralph Waldo Emerson thinks the Quakers seem to come "nearer to the sublime genius and history of Christianity than does any other sect."

A beer drinker at Louisville, Kentucky, was lately strangled by swallowing with his beverage a part of a human toe.

Hon. John P. Hale, our Minister to Spain has been convicted of smuggling goods into the country in liquidation of his accounts with the importing merchants. In other words he has abused the privileges of his official position to put money in his pocket. This is a lamentable conclusion which commenced so nobly.

## MARRIAGES

In this city, April 12, by Rev. E. R. Keys, Mr. E. S. Wormell and Miss L. Annie Packard, both of Portland.

In this city April, 14, by Rev. E. C. Bolles, Oliver E. Silsby, of Bath, and, and Mrs. E. Amanda Richardson, of Portland.

In this city, April 25, by Rev. E. C. Bolles, Isaac C. Nesmith, of Washington, D. C., and Miss Amanda C. Ricker, of Portland. [No cards.]

In this city, April 15, by Rev. E. C. Bolles, Cornelius R. Marshall and Miss Margaret B. Rose, both of Portland.

In this city, April 3, by Rev. O. T. Moulton, Merrill P. Jordan and Miss Emily E. Deering, daughter of Rufus Deering, Esq., all of Portland.

In San Francisco, January 25, 1869, by the Rev. Dr. Cox, Mr. Charles O. Babb, formerly of this city, and Miss Lucie Jones, both of Alameda, Co., Cal.

In Gorham, April 19, by the Rev. Gen. Lewis, Mr. Charles F. Robinson, of Natick, Mass., and Miss Cornelia F. Clark, of Gorham.

In the Advent Christian Chapel at Buchanan, Mich., Thursday evening, April 8, 1869, by Elder William L. Himes, Mr. Western E. Wilkinson, of Berrien, Michigan and Miss Mary F. McLellan, of Brunswick, Maine.

In Capt. Elizabeth, April 11, by Rev. A. P. Hillman, John L. Winship, of Portland and Miss Minerva T. Boucher, of Cape Elizabeth.

In Cambridge, Mass., April 7, Edwin Hadley and M. Lizzie, daughter of Edward P. Little.

In Brownfield, April 11, by Thomas Cleaves, Esq., Samuel Mason, Esq., and Mrs. Nancy Jane Floyd, both of Brownfield.

## DEATHS

In this city, April 15, Hiram A. Bowen, late Sargent Co., D. U. S. Engineers, aged 25 years.

In this city, April 16, Alice W. Carney, daughter of Hattie A. and W. C. G. Carney, aged 2 years, 4 months and 18 days.

In this city, April 5, Benjamin G. Partridge, aged 56 years.

In Westbrook, April 16, Lizze M. Lane, daughter of Josiah and Ann M. Lane, aged 7 years and 2 months.

In Porter, Feb. 10, Thomas T. Billings, only son of Samuel and Mercy Billings, aged 39 years, 10 months and 10 days.

In Saccaarappa, April 18, Mrs. Erther A., wife of David W. Babb, aged 29 years.

In Hollis, March 26, of consumption, Mrs. Martha J., wife of Samuel T. Quint, aged 22 years, 4 months, 2 days.

In North Yarmouth, April 13, Captain William T. Pierce, aged 77 years.

In Gloucester, Mass., April 11, Freddie W. Dennison, son of Capt. Charles W. Dennison, aged 5 years and 3 months.

In Auburn, April 11, Gertie Maud, daughter of Charles H. and Henrietta Staples, aged 18 months and 21 days.

At Muscatine, Iowa, April 5, 1869 of congestion, Mr. William M. Shaw, recently of Portland, Me. Aged 38 years, 9 months and 18 days. Mr. Shaw was a member and Deacon of the Central Congregational Church of Portland, Me., and though a resident with us for only a few months, by his consistent and earnest Christian living has given cheering evidence of his faith in Jesus.

He leaves a widow and two children, with many friends, grained even in his brief sojourn in this city, to mourn his loss.

Papers in Putney, Vermont, and Portland, Maine please copy.

## MEMORANDA

A DISPATCH FROM San Francisco 12th inst., states that the ship King Philip, Capt. Hubbard, from San Francisco for McKeen's Island, was nearly destroyed by fire at Honolalu (sic) on the 18th ult.

Schooner Thames, of Tremont, Capt. Robbins, broke from her anchorage at Seal Cove, 30th ult., and went ashore at Herriman's Cove, Brooklyn.

## PORTLAND TRANSCRIPT

### April 24, 1869

The Farmington Chronicle tells a bear story. Mr. Hiram Ladd, an old fox hunter and a lad came across a bear's den near Old Blue Mountain, which the former proceeded to explore and found it to contain a bear and three cubs. The second shot killed the old one, and the young ones were captured. The bear measured six feet from her nose to her tail, three and a half feet high, and weighed over 200 pounds. The cubs, with their dead mother, were taken down to Augusta, to see the sights.

A correspondent informs us that Miss Martha Holmes, of Freeport, the young lady who recently suffered severe exposure during a fit of illness, under the skillful treatment of Dr. W. H. True, of Freeport, is now doing well, though she had been given up by the first physicians of New York and Boston.

On Saturday week, Mr. Herrick Ham, of Lewiston, was picked up intoxicated in the street of that city and taken to the lockup, and placed in a cell. About 11 o'clock that night the officers went to his cell and found him dead on the floor, he having suffocated in his vomit, as we learn from the Journal.

Mr. J. Lamb, of Calais, while visiting his timber lot on the Megalloway River, a few weeks since, was kicked by one of his horses imprinting the shoe on the side of his face. He was taken up for dead, but after some time regained his senses, though he remained in a feeble state.

Mr. Charles Littlefield, conductor on the Portland & Rochester Railroad, had the heel of his foot badly crushed on Tuesday week, by falling under a car at Center Waterboro'.

Solomon Hall, of Lincoln, lost all his buildings and stock, the latter, consisting of eleven head of cattle and some sheep, by fire, on Monday week. Insured for $550.

Velocipede shoes are the latest novelty.

The store of Isaac Merrill, in North Yarmouth, was entered on Wednesday night of last week and robbed of ribbons and money to the amount of nearly $150.

The store of Levi Cram at Morrill's Corner, Westbrook, was entered on Tuesday night, of last week and robbed of fifteen dollars.

The dwelling house of Capt. Henry C. Dean, of Oxford, was destroyed by fire on Saturday, 10th inst. Partially insured.

Leonard Andrews of Biddeford, was severely injured at Oldtown, on the 14th, by the explosion of a blast on a railroad cut.

John Crowley, of East Machias, lost his house, barn, a horse, two cows, hay and farming tool, by fire on the 19th inst.

The carriage shop of P. F. Kilgore of Newry, was burned on Thursday week, with all it contents.

Robert Kelley, of Lubec, writes us that he has a Washington cent of the date 1783.

On Tuesday week, George McCurdy, stage driver between Bangor and Calais, was thrown from his seat near Wesley, and his foot getting entangled in the coach, he was dragged four miles, the horses running away until they came to the place where they change horses, when the situation of the driver was discovered. He was fatally injured. The marks were plainly visible, where he had been dragged along the road, and his watch, wallet, &c., where found scattered about as they had fallen from his pockets.

Young Marston, again went over the dam at Augusta on Friday, but this time in company with Major Frank Davis. They made the trip, but the boat upset in the surf and they had a terrible struggle to save their lives. Another boat went to their rescue, but Marston saved their lives with the aid of his paddle.

In the Superior Court, Portland, Mrs. Julia F. Cooley obtained a verdict against the town of Westbrook, for $65,000 damages, for injuries sustained on the 24th of December last, in being thrown out of a sleigh in consequence of an obstruction or defect in a highway in that town.

Parties are taking measures to test the extent of the vein of tin ore discovered on the farm of Benjamin Furbur, in Winslow. The Waterville Mail says if the deposit is as extensive as there is reason to expect, the discovery is of immense value.

Young Marston took another plunge over the Kennebec dam, at August, on Fast Day, and had the good luck to come out all right. He is evidently ambitious of becoming the champion plunger.

Fannie Patch, a little daughter of Jesse E. Patch, at Kittery, broke her leg about half way between the knee and ankle, while playing with her companions on Friday.

Mrs. Susan Jones dropped dead at the residence of her brother, Simon Tebbetts, in Sanford, on Thursday week.

The house of J. E. Leighton, in Bangor, was robbed on the 10th inst., of over $4000 in money, bonds and notes.

Mr. James Colly, of Penobscot, was thrown from his carriage on Saturday week, and had his spine badly injured.

Dr. C. W. Whitmore, of Gardiner, was thrown from his carriage last week and quite severely injured.

Widow Van Coot, is a licensed Methodist preacher in New York, and the conference there has been agitated by the question of allowing her to continue in the pastoral work. It is said that nearly 200 persons have been converted under her ministrations the past year-pretty good evidence that she has the right to preach.

Over 500,000 men are employed on the railways in the United States.

Colonel Charles O. Rogers, proprietor of the Boston Journal, died in Boston, on Wednesday week, at the age of fifty years.

The late John Minor Botts had a signet ring made of filings from the old Independence Bell in Philadelphia, and at his death he bequeathed it to General Grant, to whom it has just been duly presented.

Mrs. Twitchell declares her innocents of her mother's murder, and says she ceased visiting her husband in prison because he importuned her to confess that she committed the murder in order to save him.

A disheartened lover near Vicksburg by the name of Cushing, shot and killed the fair lady, named Andrews, who rejected him, after which he engaged in a duel with the enraged brother of the murdered lady, which resulted in the killing of both parties.

## EARLY TIMES IN MAINE

In a correspondence I have lately had with the venerable William Allen, of Norridgewock, he has favored me with is recollection of early scenes in the history of our state, which I think will be interesting to your readers. The first sketch relates to the Bingham lands, which long occupied the attention of speculators and have been a source of large wealth to proprietors, purchasers and the state.

Mr. Allen, who was long an agent in the management of these lands, was a native of Martha's Vineyard, Mass., where he was born April 16, 1780, on what was then the manor of Tisbury. In 1792, he came with his father to Maine, and established himself in the wilderness where now is the town of Industry, in Franklin County.

Their location was a log camp two miles beyond any human habitation, and forty miles beyond any incorporated town. The family lived in camp eight years, and was composed of the father, mother and ten children. William, when of age took some wild land, cleared a farm, and by his industry was able to lay aside money enough to pay his board for six weeks at the Hallowell Academy, there being no advantages for schooling any where near his abode. He improved this opportunity so earnestly that he obtained a certificate from Samuel Moody, his distinguished teacher, that he was competent to teach the branches usually taught in a common English school. He humorously says, "On my way home I had an applications for teaching two of the best schools in the county, ragged as I was." From this time his progress was onward as teacher, surveyor, selectman and assessor, Justice of the Peace, a busy trial justice, member of the Separation Conventions of Brunswick, 1816 and at Portland 1819, and 1825 and 1828 he represented Norridgewock in the legislature. He filled the office of Selectman twenty-two years and clerk of the Court of the Common Pleas twelve years, and was twenty-eight years employed in the agency of the Bingham lands. In 1849 he published a history of Norridgewock. He is now at the age eighty-nine years, enjoying a ripe and sound old age in the full possession of his intellectual faculties, ever actively employed, and has the high satisfaction of a well spent life, over which he may look without dread and with our remorse. The discipline, experience and results of such a life have a deep moral significance, and its retrospect of its stirring events cannot fail having a deep interest. W. W.

# PORTLAND TRANSCRIPT

## May 22, 1869

The Seaside Oracle says that Abner S. Hiscock, of Damariscotta, a returned soldier who lost his right arm in the Union Army, recently went into the woods and with his remaining arm, and entirely unassisted, felled, cut and split ten feet of hard wood in eight hours and a half. He has learned to write a fair round, legible hand, though not naturally left handed.

Lizzie, daughter of Zemro Hall, of Harrington, about five years old, in the absence of her mother from the room laid some bread on the stove, and attempting to brush it off with her apron, it took fire, and the child was so burned that she died in a few hours. She had strength to tell her mother how it occurred and said, "it is well with me."

While Lovell Busher, of Freedom, was cleaning his gun the other day, which had been loaded by a younger brother without his knowledge, it accidentally exploded, and three balls passed through his thigh, inflicting a very severe wound.

In Rockland, Tuesday week, Samuel Springer, while quarrying limestone, was thrown eight or ten feet into the air by a premature explosion, and his left leg was so completely smashed as to render amputation necessary. There were hopes of his recovery.

On Saturday, 8th inst., the grist mill and saw mill at Hollis Center, owned by John F. Plaisted, were destroyed by an incendiary fire. Insured.

Mr. David Young, of Rockland, a lame man, fell from a wagon, last week and broke his lame leg midway between the knee and hip.

On Sunday week, the house of Moses Freeman, in Brunswick was destroyed by fire, with nearly all the contents, Insured $800.

Mr. David Ames, a Rockland quarryman, was very badly burned last week, by a premature explosion of a seam blast.

Mr. Ephriam S. Blake, of Bangor broke his ankle very badly on Tuesday week, by falling from a step ladder and died from the effects of it on Saturday.

E. N. Hurd, of South Parkman, broke his leg the other day while trying to raise a fallen horse.

In Bath, last week, Edward Larrabee was thrown from a horse and had his right leg broken.

Mr. J. P. Morse, of Bath, has given $1000 to the Soldier's Orphan Home Fund.

A serious accident occurred on the P. S. & P. Railroad, between North and South Berwick stations on Wednesday week. Owing the displacement of a rail, the engine, baggage, mail, smoking and passenger cars of the morning up train ran off the track, piling upon and smashing each other in the most fearful manner. The shock was tremendous. Freeman Lamphrey, baggage master, was so terribly injured that he died in an hour; his remains were taken to his home in Hampton, N. H. Albert Dodge, engineer badly scalded, was brought back to Cape Elizabeth. Joseph Reed, and Charles Cram, brake-men, were slightly injured. Of the passengers, Mrs. E. A. Stevens of Saco, and a gentleman, name unknown, each had a leg broken. Mr. Charles Coe of this city, was badly bruised and one of his wrists crushed, and others were bruised and wrenched. The postal car was forced through and over the baggage car, and the hind passenger car was forced six feet directly into the smoking car, in which were six gentleman, all of who were bruised. Conductor Payson Tucker, and Superintendent Chase, did all that was possible for the relief of the wounded. It was thought that the rails were torn up by some malicious person, the spikes being drawn and thrown out on the side of the track.

On Monday week, John Reynolds, brake-man on P. S. & P. Railroad was badly jammed between the cars at Burke's Crossing and falling on the track had his leg torn open nearly up to the thigh. He was taken to his residence in this city and well cared for.

The Gardiner Reporter says David White, Jr., of Pittston, died quite suddenly on Monday week, from the effects of green paint. He had painted the blinds of the house and let them stand in his sleeping apartment to dry, applying several coats of paint.

News have been received at Bath of the death of Capt. James Lincoln, of ship Frank Maria on the passage from Batavia to London. Capt. Lincoln was a son of Eben Lincoln, Esq., of Bath, and about 30 years old.

While pretending to take care of Mr. Albert Dodge, the engineer who was so badly scalded at the accident on the Portsmouth, Saco and Portland Railroad on Wednesday, some scoundrel stole his watch.

The United State court at Charlestown, West Virginia has just given a decision in favor of ex-Senator Morrill of this state, by which his title to a large quantity of land in West Virginia is established.

Elmer Beveridge, of Rockland, a lad 14 years old, hanged himself on Friday week. It is thought the deed may have been accidentally done, while playing with the suspended rope.

William Warren, was drowned in Vinal Haven Beach, on Wednesday week, by the upsetting of a boat. He was a married man, about 25 years old, living at Vinal Haven.

The building at South Paris, belonging to Merrill's foundry, in which castings were done, was entirely destroyed by fire Friday morning. It was insured for $1500.

An Augusta boy named Holt, got into a scuffle and drew a knife with which he made a bad gash in his opponent's thigh. Holt was arrested.

Ambrose Scammon, of Franklin, lost his house by fire on Thursday week. Little saved, and small insurance.

"Rev." John R. Smith has been held to trial at Bath in the sum of $5000, on a charge of forgery.

Mrs. Caleb Barker, of Pittston is a smart old lady now in her ninetieth year, yet still able to read without spectacles, and to make up forty yards of sheeting into sheets and pillow cases in one week.

Joseph Levensaler, of Sebec, was killed on Thursday week by falling off a new barn frame that he was helping to raise. He leaves a wife and two small children.

Young Patterson, of Belfast, who has been sentenced to three years in the State Prison, will meet there Blake, the murderer of his father.

The dwelling house of Mrs. Fisher, on Cushnoc Heights, Bangor, Maine, was totally destroyed by fire on Friday night. Loss $1000; no insurance.

A daughter of Orin Richardson, thirteen years old, was drowned at Milford, on Monday week, while playing near the main sluice of the mills.

The Biddeford Journal says a human skeleton was dug up under an old building in the rear of that office last week. There was no appearance of a coffin. There is a tradition that a man residing there suddenly disappeared a long time ago.

Capt. John Lowry of Kittery Point, watchman of the Navy Yard, fell and broke his arm at that place on Friday, suffering a compound fracture.

A Prince to whom the daughter of an American family in Paris was about to be married, has turned out bogus. Another "caution" to ambitious American mammas who sell their daughters for European titles.

Henry Ward Beecher once stated that he had made loans to individuals from all over the country. He had never known his money to come back except in one instance, and that was when he loaned $3 to a poor Negro woman.

Dr. Plumer, formerly of this city, inventor of the anatomical last, died at the Massachusetts General Hospital in Boston, last week, after a short illness.

Schooner, D. C. Webb was struck by lightning on the 3rd inst., off Cape Hatteras, and all hand were prostrated. All recovered except David Knight, of Deer Isle, Me., brother of the Captain who was instantly killed.

Elecampane root is the latest remedy for the bite of a mad dog.

General Thomas has refused the gift of a silver service from his army comrades, on the ground that he is determined never to receive a donation under any circumstances. A rule that our public men generally would do well to follow.

Mr. D. S. Masterman of Weld, shot a bear recently that weighed 415 pounds, and measured seven feet in length.

Joseph Hellinger, a farmer in Stephen County, Indiana, ploughed up an old boot the other day, in which his little son found $300 in gold and silver coin.

The English papers all criticize Senator Sumner's speech on the Alabama claim-but none of them published it!

## MARRIAGES

In Woburn, Mass., May 13th by Rev. H. C. Townley, Mr. Deblois N. Binford, of Cambridge, formerly of Baldwin, Me., and Miss Isadora F. Teasdale of Winchester, Mass.

In Cedar Rapids, Iowa, April 24th, by Rev. D. H. Cooley, Daniel W. Barker and Miss Martha J. Burkar, both of Cedar Rapids.

At the Methodist parsonage, Scotland, May 2nd., by Rev. J. A. Strout, James S. J. Skilling, of Cape Elizabeth, and Rhoda P. Emery of York.

In Cornish, March 1st., by Rev. A. Cole, Emerson Kimball and Miss Clara E. Kimball, both of Hiram.

In this city, Mary 12th by Rev. O. T. Moulton, Benjamin W. Stover and Miss Julia Sampson, all of Portland.

In this city, May 12th, Joseph Coolidge and Miss M. Ella Hill, both of Portland.

In this city, May 14th, Sylvanus B. Hamilton, and Miss Maria L. Crooker, both of Portland.

In this city, May 10th, Augustus F. Hannaford, of Boston Heights and Miss Sarah A. Walden, of Portland.

In this city, May 7th, Mark H. Sawyer, of Portland, and Miss Marcia McRonald of Cape Elizabeth.

In this city, May 16th, Edmund L. Walker and Miss Annie E. Thomas, also Lendall G. L. Foote and Miss Francis A. McGowen of Portland.

In this city, May 17th, Isreal T. McIntire and Miss Francis M. Huston, both of Portland.

In this city, May 26th, James E. Hatch of Portland and Miss Mary E. Oram, of St. John.

In Chicago, Ill., May 19th, P. R. Hilton, of Chicago and Miss Agnes O. Ricker of Portland.

In Gorham, May 10th , Dana Plummer of Gorham, and Miss Clara J. Sargent, of Hollis.

In Berlin, Wis., April 20th, James Hargrave of Fair Water, Wis., and Miss Martha Warren of Gorham, Me.

In Dixfield, May 1st, Albert S. Austin, of Canton, and Ella J. Austin, of Dixfield, also L. C. Willoughby and Almena S. Austin.

In Augusta, May 6th., William Leighton and Mary E. Clark.

In Boston, April 17th Elish B. Taylor of Buckfield and Miss Emma J. Forbes, of Paris.

## DEATHS

In Norway, May 13th Mercy Ann Lida, eldest daughter of John and Emeline Frost, aged 15 years.

In Waterville, April 10th, Ellen S. Boothby, aged 21 years, 10 months.

In Brookline, Mass., May 9th, Addie V., daughter of O. and A. V. Benner, 9 months.

In this city, May 12th, Albert S. Jackson, aged 30.

In this city, May 11th Isabel W. only child of John E. and Sarah E. Strong, aged 13 months.

In this city, May 16th, Joseph Dale, of Saco, aged 70.

In this city, May 10th, Lizzie Eben, daughter of T. S. and U. C. McConky, aged 6 year, 7 months and 17 days.

In this city, May 17th, Henry M., son of David B. and Mary Fuller, aged 8 months and 15 days.

In this city, May 13th, Mrs. Nancy Waterhouse, aged 74.

In this city, May 13th, Henry Nowell, aged 72.

In this city, May 10th, Mrs. Eunice Evans, aged 85.

In this city, Alice F., only daughter of William and Annie White, aged 13 months.

In Boston, May 17th Mrs. Margaret, widow of Henry Reed, formerly of Damariscotta, Me., aged 63.

In Gorham, May 12, Edith R. Day, aged 16.
In Lewiston, May 11, Mrs. Mary A. Templeton, aged 49.
In Freeport, May 5th, Mrs. Martha W. Griffin, aged 91.
In Harpswell, May 8th, Fannie J. Benson, aged 16.
In Boston, May 12th, Dr. J. C. Plumer, aged 43
In North Waterford, May 7th, Deacon Amos Gage, aged 72.
In East Jay, April 26th, Mrs. Louisa Sturdivant, aged 24.
In Farmington, April 19th., Mrs. Eliza Holley, aged 81.
In Washington, D. C., Mrs. Maria F., wife of George S. Berry, of Damariscotta, aged 29.
In Auburn, April 8th Mrs. S. Maria Tracey, aged 50.
In Augusta, May 6th, Paul Stickney, aged 75.
In Gardiner, May 13th, James Tarbox, aged 85.
In Hartland, May 6th, Winthrop A. Hight, aged 80.

MEMORANDA

Key West, May 10th-brig Omaha, was capsized 1st inst., a. m. Capt. Toothaker and three seamen only were saved.

Schooner Smfr (?) Cherryfield, with coal, was sunk by a collision at New York, 12th.

Schooner Farragut, of Pembroke, from Windsor, N. S. for Baltimore, was wrecked at Cape Split 10th inst., crew saved.

LAUNCHED–At Searsport, 26th ult., by Capt. William McGilvery, a first class ship of 1200 tons named John C. Potter. She is owned by the builder Capt. George McClure, who is to command her.

# PORTLAND TRANSCRIPT

## May 29, 1869

A Turner correspondent of the Lewiston Journal says that a man died recently in that town of almost giant proportions, He was six feet four inches high, and weighed three hundred pounds. His name was John Keene. He was buried beside the remains of his father whose name was also John, who died at the same age (80 years,) and he also leaves a son John who is six feet six inches in height. The boards of which his coffin was made were sawed by himself for his father's coffin twenty seven years ago. There are few logs of sufficient size to furnish whole boards for such a coffin.

The post office at Madawaska has been discontinued, because no one could be found to take it. The following postmasters have been appointed: Russel B. Hazey, at Strickland's Ferry, B. F. Walton, at New Portland, at Cooper's Mills; William H. Sprague, at Orland.

At the burning of Merrill's Iron Foundry, in South Paris, Mr. John F. Jordan, foreman of Pacific Engine, was knocked down by a falling axe, which made a fearful gash near the left eye. He has since been confined to his bed, both eyes being badly inflamed.

Hiram Mace, a Farmington rum seller, after spending sixty days in jail as a common seller of liquor, came out crazy, tried to drown himself, and became so boisterous that it was necessary to send him to the Insane Hospital.

Miss. M. W. Mitchell, of Dover, a member of the present senior class at Bates College, Lewiston, will be the first woman graduate from a New England college.

A fellow named John Cook, has been bound over at Lewiston in the sum of $400 for an attempted outrage on a child seven years of age, at Wales.

Col. Smart has sold the Biddeford Democrat to Marcus and Oscar F. Watson, and is going to look after his large landed property on the Penobscot.

Charles Fish, of Patten, while at work on a drive on the Mattawamkeag, a few days since was instantly killed by being struck on the head by a log.

S. O. Libby, a photographic artist, at Augusta committed suicide on Friday night of last week, by taking poison. Financial difficulties were the cause.

In West Newfield, on the 7th inst., Mrs. Reuben Davis fell dead on the floor while at work as usual; probable cause, heart disease.

At Hallowell, on Thursday week, two little boys name Davenport and Cole, were drowned by the caving in of a wall.

On Monday, William S. Smith, a teamster was run over and almost instantly killed at the Maine Central depot, Bangor. The noise of the cars made the horses shy, causing the drive to drop his reins; when reaching to catch them he fell forward under the wheels, which passed over him, crushing in his breast and producing death in about half an hour.

On the 10th inst., a man named Maddocks in the employ of Thomas Nye, of Union, got up in the night, saying he was going to see to his horse, and has not since been heard from though his knife, with blood upon it, has been found and some hair supposed to be his whiskers.

The Lewiston Journal says that Zelotus P. Judkins, of Livermore, while in pursuit of game, on the 15th inst., by some means discharged his gun, the contents of which passed through his head, causing immediate death.

Messrs. Soule & Co., of Bangor, who are making a drive on the West Branch of the Penobscot, have lost two of their men by drowningWilliam Raney and James Dority.

Joseph Bartlett, Esq., of the Bangor Jeffersonian, has returned from his trip to the south. He does not think his trip rewarded him with any appreciable improvement in health.

Mrs. Finn, of Eastport, has been sentenced to pay a fine and go to jail for thirty days for selling liquor to a young man who was found boisterously drunk on the streets.

Jeremiah, son of Michael Shea, of Ellsworth, was strangled to death on the 14th ult., by getting the rope of a swing entangled about his neck. He was 14 years old.

Charley, son of Hiram Ladd, of Weld, a bright boy of six years, was drowned in that village, on Thursday week, while attempting to cross a brook on a log.

At the raising of a barn at Rumford, Solomon Raymond fell twenty-six feet, striking on ice, and remained insensible until he died a few days later.

The schooner, Susan Duncan, Capt. Turner, which sailed from Bangor on the 15th, for Newark, N. J., was lost on Cape Cod, in the gale of Wednesday night and all her crew are supposed to have perished. She was built at Bangor, and owned by Kelsey & Gray.

The body of Capt. Turner, late of master brig Susan Duncan, lost on Cape Cod, has washed ashore at Chatham. Nothing has been heard in regard to the crew. Capt. Turner leaves a wife, and two children in Bangor.

The Press says that widow Hannah E. Andrews, of Lovel, who was one hundred years old on the 13th of April last, has been the mother of thirteen children, and has about 170 descendants now living.

The Machias Republican says that Mr. John Young of Columbia Falls, while at work in the field plowing, May 10th, became suddenly indisposed, went into the house and died in a hour.

Lubec, in the death of Hon. Jeremiah Fowler has lost one of its oldest, and most useful and best beloved citizens.

The Jeff and Joe Davis plantation, thirty miles below Vicksburgh is leased by an old Negro at $10,000 a years. He hired 150 hands to work it. Not a white man is to been seen about the place. The whole plantation of several thousand acres is planted in cotton, which appears very promising.

President Johnson pardoned one hundred and forty-two counterfeiters and ninety-one violators of the internal revenue laws.

Earl Radnor, a Paris youth of ninety-one is dead. He remembered going through the cells of the Bastille the day after it was sacked.

The Hallowell Gazette says that Mr. Benjamin Blake, of that city, owns a cow that produced without extra feed, between March 16th and May 15, *one hundred pounds and three ounces of better*, besides furnishing the family of six persons with the amount of milk needed for the table.

Dr. James M. Bates, of Yarmouth, has been appointed an examining surgeon of the Pension Bureau.

Gov. Chamberlain will deliver the address at the New England Fair to be held this fall in Portland.

Gov. Geary has pardoned Hester Vaughn, sentenced to be hanged for child murder, and she has sailed for England.

## MARRIAGES

In Windham, May 22nd, by Rev. H. J. Bradbury, Mr. Freeland A. Staples and Miss Mary A. Senter; also by the same Mr. William C. Stapels and Miss Martha F. Libby, all of Windham.

In Cape Elizabeth, Mary 23rd, Mr. Uranus Stacey and Miss Alberta M. Libby, both of Saco.

In Gorham, May 2nd, Mr. Emery O. Walker, of Portland and Miss Nellie L. Purinton, of Gorham.

In this city, Mary 20th., Charles B. Poor, and Miss Mary J. Gatley, both of Manchester, N. H.

In this city, May 17th Joseph W. Stubbs and Miss Agnes Gigger, both of Portland.

In this city, May 17th, Simeon Cutter and Miss Josephine Kimball.

In Auburn, May 18th, Charles H. Morgan and Una L. Davis.

## DEATHS

On Peak's Island, May 21st., Mr. John Brackett, aged 75 years, 4 months and 19 days.

In Bethel, May 13th, Mrs. Deborah L. (Whitman) Thayer, aged 30th years.

In Presque Isle, May 1st., Mary Ann, wife of Stephen Nason, formerly of Westbrook, aged 54 years and 3 months.
In this city, May 23rd, Miss Mary Sawyer.
In this city, May 24, of paralysis, George McCoe, aged 40.
In this city, May 17th, Etta J. Warren, aged 10.
In Bethel, May 5th, Mrs. Mary B. Mitchell, aged 82
In Marysville, May 7th, of paralysis, Mr. Reuben Stubbs, aged 76.
In this city, May 21st, Mrs. Catherine S. Greene, aged 51.
In this city, May 17th, Henry M., son of David B. and Mary Jane Fuller, aged 8 months, 15 days.
Drowned at Santa Rosa, Union, Cuba, May 4th Edward F. Staples, of Cape Elizabeth, Me., aged 29.

## MEMORANDA

LAUNCHED-At Brunswick, 18th inst. a first class brig of 600 tons, named Isaac Lincoln. Also, 1st inst., from the yard at Varney's Mills, a fine schooner of 93 tons, named Mary L. Varney ,to be commanded by Capt. R. Dunham.

At Ellsworth, 14th inst., from the yard of I. M. Grant a schooner of 140 tons, named J. Kendedy to be commanded by Capt. L. Smith.

PORTLAND TRANSCRIPT

June 5, 1869

Business is getting to be quite brisk at Bar Mills, notwithstanding the little, "unpleasantness," in Cuba. Mr. Charles McKenney is now manufacturing about 600 pair hogs heads per day. The logs of the first drive of the season are beginning to run.

Mr. Alfred Brooks, of South Eliot, broke one of his legs in two places, on Wednesday, while using a harrow. The oxen started when he was adjusting the harrow, which caught him, threw him down, and inflicted the injury.

James Scott, Pembroke, died very suddenly Tuesday night, May 18. He ate his supper in good health, went out and soon returned complaining of a severe pain in the chest. He died in half an hour.

A match game of Base Ball was played between the Granite States of Portsmouth, N. H., and the Minnies of South Berwick, Me., on the grounds of the latter. Minnies victorious by 32 runs, Score 15 to 47.

The children of Mr. Hooker, of Gardiner were playing with matches in the loft of his stable, on Friday week, and the result was the total destruction of stable and house, with contents. No insurance.

Ezra L. Manter, of Carmel, on Monday week, fell from a ladder some twenty feet to the ground, and now lies in critical condition, his body, and lower limbs paralyzed.

The faculty at Waterville, recommend Charles F. Dunn, of Litchfield to be a cadet at West Point from the 3rd division. There were eight competitors at the examination.

The Biddeford Journal says that in the orchard owned by Mr. Jefferson Raitt, of Eliot, stand some very ancient pear trees. His grandfather, who was born in 1730, picked up and ate a pear under one of these when he was six years of age. One of these trees is two feet in diameter. Blossoms are appearing on these trees this year.

The counting house of Charles and Elias Milliken, lumber manufacturers of Augusta, was broken into on the night of the 26th inst., the safe opened and some $30,000 worth of stock, consisting of bank and Ticonic Water Power shares, carried off. The robbers went deliberately to work, and were evidently familiar with the premises.

The remains of young Delano who suddenly disappeared from Young's Corner, Auburn, two weeks ago, were found Thursday morning floating near the shore in Taylor Pond. It was evidently a case of suicide.

The Farmington Chronicle says that "B. M. Eastman, of the firm of Eastman Bros., of Portland, came to this place, Thursday, on the first through train from Sacramento, California, to Farmington, Me., making the trip in nine days."

Daniel McCully, a Scotsman 24 years old, was drowned at Upper Stillwater, on Thursday week, while at work on the logs in the mill pond.

The store of John Eveleth, in Greenville, was destroyed by fire on the 21st inst., most of the goods saved. No insurance.

The Lancaster House, at East Winthrop, was burned on Friday, together with out-buildings. The cotton factory, at Winthrop was also damaged by fire the same day.

Miss D. L. Cook, 18 years old, and of a remarkable personal beauty, formerly a resident of Maine, came to her death recently in San Francisco from taking a large dose of arsenic to improve her complexion.

The Hon. Mrs. Ane Keohokalole Kapaakkea, a high chiefess (sic) of the ancient Hawaiian race, was recently buried at Honolulu with royal honors. She once served in the Hawaiian Parliament, and was an early convert to Christianity.

Gen. Beauregard owes the United States $10.30. Uncle Sam has dunned him, but the ex-rebel presents an old claim in offset.

John W. Randall of Portland, came out second best in the three mile scull race with Butler, of Newburgh, N. Y., which came off at Boston, last Monday.

## MARRIAGES

In Bristol, May 27th, by Rev. P. Rowell, George W. Thurston and Mrs. Mary E. Sprowl, both of Bristol.

In Saccarappa, May 27th, by Rev. H. J. Bradbury, Charles M. Stuart, of Windham, and Miss Rebecca J. Ingersoll, of Falmouth.

In Bowdoinham May 22nd, by Rev. E. Purington, Hiram Frost and Miss Esther V. Adams, both of Bowdoinham.

In Bethel, May 28th, by Rev. David Garland, C. E. Chapman, of Portland, and Miss Fannie E., daughter of T. H. Chapman, Esq., of Bethel.

In East Pittston, May 13th at the residence of the bride's father by Rev. J. I. Brown, James E. Matthews of Boothbay, and Nellie T. Brown of East Pittston.

In Westboro' Mass., by Rev. Dr. Flanders, Mr. Charles I. W. Robinson, of Island Falls, Me., and Miss S. A. Sibley, of Westboro'.

In this city, May 26th, Fred J. J. Smith of Portland, and Miss Lydia M. Johnson, of Falmouth.

In this city, May 26th, Joseph Lee and Susan Johnson, both of Portland.

In Sweden, May 12th, by Rev. D. B. Byther, J. Perley Barker, of Portland, and Miss Mary F. Smart, of Sweden.

## DEATHS

In Salem, May 9th, Mary Wood, wife of Henry Davidson aged 28 years, 9 months.

In Flushing N. Y., May 10th Henry W. Scott, 1st Assistant Engineer, U. S. Navy aged 30 years, son of Capt. Andrew Scott, formerly of this city.

In this city, May 26th, Lena Florence True, aged 8 years.

In this city, May 25th, Nettie C. Hill, aged 8 years.

In this city, May 28th, Mr. Sarah Tobey, aged 85.

In this city, May 23rd, Mrs. Abby Kennard, aged 68.

In this city, May 29th, James O. Harmon, aged 40.

In Windham, May 19th, Mr. Ephraim Legrow, aged 67 years, 6 months. In the death of Mr. Legrow a worthy citizen, a faithful husband, an indulgent father and a kind neighbor has passed away. In all these relation in life he stood pre–eminent. In 1854 he represented Windham in the Legislature and for several successive years he was a selectman of the town. In him the unfortunate found a friend most sympathizing and helpful. Towards others his conduct was what he would have others be to him. He believed in God our kind heavenly Father and in his Son, Jesus Christ as our merciful and divine Savior. The wife of his youth, now well stricken in years, with whom he had walked more than forty years in the greatest cheerfulness and affection, together with a family of eight children and a large circle of friends, mourn his loss. All these will hold his memory in grateful affection, and upon them may the mantle of his integrity and the benevolence of his disposition abide continually.

## PORTLAND TRANSCRIPT

### June 12, 1869

In Biddeford, on Monday week, a hatchet fell from a building upon the foot of Mr. Thomas Chick, making an ugly wound and cutting off deep arteries. Same day Mr. Ai Clark, while turning his team, became entangled in the wheels, and had his knee dislocated–an injury of rare occurrence, some authorities asserting, says the Journal, that the knee never becomes dislocated.

Jesse G. Sprague of Charlotte, writes to the Eastport Sentinel that he killed a bear on the 28th ult., that has been doing mischief in that town for years. He caught him in a trap that had a heavy chain and clog attached, which he dragged a mile before he was shot. It took five men to get him out of the woods. His head weighs twenty pounds, and his skin covers thirty square feet.

Mr. Sleeper, proprietor of a hotel in Houlton, was recently attacked and severely beaten by a man named Keefe; his face was badly pounded and some of his ribs broken. Keefe left for the Provinces, and Sleeper is confined to his bed.

At Bangor, on Saturday week, Capt. Darby, of schooner William Stevens, of Belfast, dropped dead on the deck of his vessel. The moment before he was in apparently good health.

As Mr. Abel Fletcher, of Sumner, was returning from a funeral when he was thrown from his carriage and had two of his ribs and collar bone broken.

In Starks, recently, Widow Greaton aged 83 years, was so shockingly burned by her clothes taking fire, that she died a few days after.

The house of Benjamin Oliver in Bath was entered by burglars Tuesday week and quite a variety of articles taken.

An Irishman named Downey, was drowned in the Penobscot River on Monday week.

On Tuesday week, a boat containing nine men, belonging to Dunn's drive, was carried over a small fall below Rumford Falls. Five jumped out, two of whom were saved and three drowned. The four remaining in the boat went over in safety. The name of the men drowned were Edward Graw, of Eddington, Charles Flint of Oldtown, and Michael Gibbon, of Bangor.

Indication now are that the choice of the Republican convention for Governor will rest between Governor Chamberlain and Hon. Sidney Perham. Governor Chamberlain's friends are pressing his claims persistently, while Mr. Perham will got into the convention with strong support.

The residence of Dr. S. L. Cole, of Hallowell, was partly destroyed by fire about 4 o'clock Saturday morning, The fire was first discovered in the barn and rear part of the house, supposed to have taken from a train passing late on Friday evening.

At Medway, on Sunday week a little girl, daughter of Charles Wharton, five years old, was drowned in the river.

In Brunswick, Tuesday week, Mr. Barton R. Jordan, had his right leg broken by a kick from a runaway horse.

Mrs. Hannah Yeaton of Oxford is 84 years old and last season spun 240 skeins of yarn and wove 212 yards of cloth besides doing house work. The year previous she spun 365 skeins of yarn and wove 200 yards of cloth. She spun 53 skeins of fine woolen yarn and wove it into 10 ½ yards of full cloth that weighted 5 lbs. 2oz., which she helped make into garment for men's wear and received first premium last year for checked flannel that she made. She is a constant subscriber and reader of the Transcript that is always paid for in advance.

The Press learns that a deaf and dumb man name George Curtis, a farmer much respected and residing with his son near New Gloucester station, was struck by an engine while walking on the track, and was so badly injured that he died an hour afterwards.

Col. John Hale, of Madison, has planted twenty acres of potatoes this year.

One Mrs. Jane B. Sawyer, liquor seller, of Jonesport, who twice stole a barrel of her own whiskey, after it had been seized by the officers, substituting water therefor, has been bound over to the Supreme Court on a charge of larceny.

Mr. Silas Tripp, of Raymond, about 50 years of age, committed suicide by hanging himself in his barn last Friday, while laboring under a temporary fit of insanity.

Dennis Reen, a convicted murderer, committed suicide last Sunday, in the jail at East Cambridge, Mass.

It seems that even in the matter of personal vanity, man may claim full equality with woman. The case of the Maine girl in California, who died from an over-dose of arsenic which she took to improve her beauty, is matched by that of Sir Frederick Bruce, who it is said, died from devotion to his complexion, which he took arsenic to improve.

## MARRIAGES

In Waldoboro' June 2nd, by Rev. C. Packard, Eugene H. Wade, and Miss Oliver E. Stahl, both of Waldoboro'.

In this city, June 2, by Rev. E. C. Boles, Storer S. Knight, and H. Lizzie Leavit, daughter of C. H. Greene, Esq., all of this city.

In this city, June 3rd, Thomas L. Heirlighy and Miss Nettie J. Bell, both of Portland.

In this city, June 1st., John J. Shehan and Miss Margaret O' Connell, both of Portland.

In this city, May 29th, Alexander H. Fairbanks and Miss Harriet Saunders, both of Portland.

In this city, June 5th, Robert Hunter and Miss Caroline A. Chamberlain, both of Portland.

In this city, June 5th, Albert L. Rand, and Miss Mary A. Mayo, both of Standish.

In Lewiston, May 27th, William F. Pitman and Matilda A. King.

In Boson, June 2nd, John T. Bullock, of North New York, and Miss Sarah E. Bryant, of Westbrook.

In Lewiston, June 2nd, John Booth and Elizabeth Garlic.

## DEATHS

In Centreville, Cal., May 4th, Mrs. Maria A. Babb, wife of J.W. Babb, formerly of this city, aged 54.

In this city, May 31st., Rev. Charles Soule, aged 74.

In this city, May 31st., Charles Wells, of Omaha, aged 38.
In this city, June 2nd, Mrs. Margaret J. Fuller, aged 34.
In this city, June 5th, Mrs. Jane Hoyt, aged 61.
In this city, June 7th, Abiel Somerby, aged 59.
In this city, June 6th, Mrs. Susie M. Hubbs, aged 29.
In Biddeford, June 6th, George Edwin Small, cashier of the First National Bank, aged 42 years 11 months.
In North Yarmouth, May 30th, Joseph Morse, aged 83.
In Woolwich, June 3rd, Mrs. Charlotte Buck, aged 80.
In Gardiner, June 4th, Mrs. Louisa A. Johnson, aged 42.
In Solon, May 22nd, Mrs. Betsey French, aged 83.
In Gardiner, May 23rd, Joseph Mitchell, aged 70.
In Freeport, May 28, Mrs. Hannah A. Litchfield, aged 87.
In Bath, May 28th, Hugh Rogers, aged 64.
In Bath, May 30th, Miss Sarah D. Riggs, aged 38.
In Westbrook, May 30th, Mrs. Sarah A. Dalton, aged 67.
In Westbrook, June 1st, James Kidder, aged 63.
In Westbrook, June 3rd, Calvin Whitcomb.

In Shelburne, N. H., May 25th, Jacob Stevens, aged 79. Guileless he lived on earth patiently laboring in the path of duty. Trustingly, in sickness, he bowed to Heaven's will, which he ever acknowledged as supreme. Death disarmed of its sting–the grave of its victory, and had no terrors for him. Softly the celestial gates unfolded and gently the waiting spirit passed to its reward of rest and peace. [City papers please copy.]

## MEMORANDA

Brig Machias went ashore at Abacoa 1st ult., started keel and sprung leak, and was obliged to throw overboard part of deck load log wood to get the vessel afloat.

LAUNCHED–At Bath, 27th a barque of 983 tons, named Niphon to be commanded by Capt. A. P. Boyd.

At Saco, 29th, by Capt. Hartley, a schooner of 250 tons.

At Calais recently from the yard of O. B. Rideout, a schooner of 222 tons, named the Mary T. Trundy, to be commanded by Capt. J. C. Warren, of Deer Isle.

Schooner Victory, of Ellworth, with lumber was run into 3rd inst., a.m. by steamer Aries from Boston for Philadelphia, cutting her down and causing her to fill. The schooner was towed into Provincetown.

## PORTLAND TRANSCRIPT

### June 19 1869

George F. Cox, a disabled soldier, from the "Soldier's Home," at Augusta, fell into the Kennecbec from a tug boat and was drowned last week. He was subject to fits, and fell overboard while suffering from an attack.

Charles A. Stevens, of Norway, receives the prize of excellence in composition and declamation, awarded at the Senior exhibition of Bowdoin College, for the class of 1869.

The residence of John Berry, postmaster of Gardiner, was struck by lightning on the afternoon of the 8th inst., The house was somewhat damaged, but no one was injured.

Wesley Newton, of Industry, was seriously injured by being thrown from his carriage at Farmington depot on the 7th inst. His horse was frightened by the cars.

George E. Small, cashier of the First Nation Bank of Biddeford, who died last week, was formerly a resident of this city, and is mourned by a large circle of friends.

The barn of Mr. Jordan, at South Auburn was burned on Sunday week; eleven tons of hay and three pigs were among the contents. No Insurance.

A child of Emery and Margaret Moon, of Hancock, four years old, was burned to death from playing with matches, on the 3rd inst.

F. W. Brown, of Augusta, pays a tax of nearly $15 on a pig, which is valued by the city assessors at $500.

Mr. John Dunton, of Augusta, formerly a resident in Bath, committed suicide last Saturday by throwing himself upon the railroad track as a gravel train was passing. He had been suffering from mental derangement for several weeks, and had been closely watched.

The "Voice," started at Sherman Mills two years ago, by a boy eleven years old, is said to be now a permanent, and flourishing paper, still published by Willie Sleeper, and edited hereafter by Mr. J. W. Caldwell.

Mr. Morrill, of Corinth, went to his barn to milk the cows on the 8th inst. He was soon after found there in a dying condition, supposed to have been injured by the cattle.

The farm buildings of Stephen Giles, of Thorndike, were destroyed by fire last week Sunday. Loss, $2500; no insurance.

Edwin Booth was married last week to Miss McVicker, who recently been playing Juliet to his Romeo.

Isaac Harris, who made the masts of the famous old frigate Constitution, died last week in Boston, aged 90 years.

President Grant and family were on a train which ran over a cow at Annapolis, Md., on the 9th inst., several passengers were seriously injured but no one killed. It was a very narrow escape as the train was on an embankment twenty feet high.

Stephen Henry Chase, Esq., District Judge of Nevada, formerly of Fryburg in this state, has become insane and been taken to the asylum at Stockton, Cal. The sad death of his wife, who was a native of this city, well be remembered by thousands of readers. Mr. Chase was expected east this season, on a visit to his friends. He was President of the Senate of Maine in 1847.

About one eighth of all the voters of the town of Stratham, N. H., was blessed with the name of Wiggin.

Miss Amanda Craig has obtained a verdict of $100,000 in a breach of promise case against a Mr. Sprague of Chicago. Sprague, who is a wealthy man, took out his false teeth, dressed meanly and made a hideous appearance, in court, in order to make the jury believe Miss Craig never *could* have loved him for anything but his money. His lawyer also made this the principal point of their arguments, that their client was such a monster that no decent woman could love for anything but his money, or even respect him! Their attempts to prove she was *not* a decent woman, by no direct evidence except that of the monster, their client, was the most unfortunate part of their strange defense. Miss Craig is a teacher in a public school of Cincinnati.

## MARRAIGES

In this city, June 12th, by Rev. O. T. Moulton, Cyrus H. Eaton, and Miss Annie M. Lewis, all of Portland.

In this city, June 14th, Thomas C. Hudson and Miss Theodora B. Jones, both of Westbrook.

In Gorham, June 13th, by Rev. H. B. Abbott, Edward R. Harmon and Miss Lydia Trask, both of Westbrook.

In Kennebunkport at the Methodist Church, by the Rev. Daniel Halleron, Rev. Roscoe Sanderson, of Portland and Miss Addie W. Luques, of Kennbunkport.

In Gorham, N.H., June 6th, by Rev. H. B. Mitchell, Oliver H. McKeen and Miss Annie M. Bailey, both of Gorham.

In this city, June 6th, by Rev. O. T. Moulton, Elias Harris and Miss Rebecca Brown, both of Westbrook.

In this city, June 7th, John Wark and Miss Elizabeth Sharp, both of Portland.

In this city, June 8th, Charles B. Baker, of Brunswick and Miss M. Lucretia Chase, of Portland.

In this city, June 8th, Newell W. Edson and Miss Mary W. Morrison, both of Portland.

In this city, June 8th, Charles H. Knowlton and Ella Carroll, daughter of James S. Staples.

In this city, June 9th, William E. Strout and Miss Dora B. Russell, both of Portland. (No cards.)

In this city, June 9th, James E. Fallon, and Carrie, only daughter of James Berry, both of Portland.

In this city, June 10th, George H. Weeks, and Miss Georgiana Hamilton.

In Ellsworth June 4th, Hosea T. Harper, of Boston, and Miss Emma H. Richardson, of Mt. Desert.

In Phipsburg, June 6th , James Harris and Mrs. Elizabeth S. Wallace.

In Gardiner, June 8th, Walter J. Wood, of Rockland, and Julia O. Davis, of Gardiner.

In New York, June 2nd, David H. Drummond, Esq., of this city, and Nina Van Renselaer Finlay, of N. Y.

In Boston, May 26th, William Richardson, Esq., and Sophia L. Chaffee, daughter of the late Capt. Martin Gerts, of Portland.

In Baltimore, June 8th George F. Junkins of this city and Miss Georgia M. Waldron, of Baltimore.

In Boston, June 8th, Capt. James S. Otis, of Brunswick and Miss Nettie W. Whittier, of this city.

In Mechanic Falls, May 30th, Henry W. Pierce and Louise A. Curtis, both of Paris.

In Scarboro', June 9th, Charles B. Garey, Saco and Miss Lemyra C. Waterhouse, of Scarboro'.

In Bath, June 2, Charles J. Johnson, of New York, and Clara Augusta P. Larrabee, of Bath.

In Ellsworth, May 26th, Horace Holman and Mrs. Betsey R. Elliot.

In North Montville, May 27th, Oliver Bowen, Jr., of Knox and Margaret F. Watts, of Montville.

In Westbrook, June 9th, Oscar W. Sargent and Miss Jennie M. Waite, both of Westbrook.

## DEATHS

In Standish, May 21st, William H. Lombard, aged 19 years, 9 months.

In this city, June 14th, Willie H. only child of Lewis B. and Mary A. Eustis, aged 2 years, 9 months,

In this city, June 9th, Albert S. Foster, aged 29

In this city, June 7th, Wesley Oliver, aged 31.

In this city, June 11th, Abbie Waterhouse, aged 13.

In this city, June 12th, Mrs. Esther Rich, aged 90.

In this city, June 12th, Ida E. Syms, aged 13.

In Belfast, May 19th, Mrs. Polly Patterson, age 86.

In Warren, May 27th, Calvin S. Wetherbee.

In Waldo, June 8th, Henry J. Woods, aged 76.

In Rockland, June 3rd, Miss Lizzie J. Kelley, age 76.

In Turner, May 28th, Mrs. Abigail Durgin, aged 49.

In Saco, May 23rd, Mrs. Susan Small, aged 36.

In Kennebunk, April 22, George W. Hardy, aged 55.

In Kennebunk, May 26th, Mrs. Emma W. Oakes, 19

In Kennebunk, May 19th, Dr. Nicholas E. Smart, aged 67.

In Bath, May 30th, Miss Sarah D. Riggs, aged 38.

In Bowdoin, May 29th, Mrs. Elizabeth Snow, aged 61.

In Sumner, May 29th Mrs. Narcissa Sewall, aged 74 daughter of the venerable Father Samuel Sewall.

In Exeter, June 5th Hon. Amasa Stetson, age 67.

In Cape Elizabeth, May 25th, William Parker, age 31.
In Augusta, June 4th, Charles Going, aged 55, an inmate of the Insane Hospital.
In Windsor, June 1st, Sarah F. Taylor, aged 36
In Jay, May 12th, Isaac West, aged 15.
In Rockland, June 6th, Deborah E. Miller, aged 12.
In Shapleigh, May 27th, Mrs. Mary R. Ham, aged 44.
In West Paris, June 5th, Mrs. Linnie H. Lock, aged 22.
In Bath, June 11th, Miss Vesta A. Blaisdell, aged 19.
In Industry, Mary 3rd, James E. Thompson, aged 19.
In Gouldboro', May 17th, Mrs. Sarah Guptill, aged 96.
In Roxbury, April 23, Charles H. Robbins, aged 40.

## PORTLAND TRANSCRIPT

### June 26, 1869

William B. Rackliff, of Stark, was arrested several years ago for the crime of rape upon the mother of his step-mother, He escaped the officers, and enlisted in the regular army; was discharged when his term of enlistment expired, returned to his former home and has now been re-arrested and lodged in Norridgewock jail.

Mr. Longley, a harness maker of Lewiston, has had three of his late workmen arrested for robbing him of material from his shop. Two, named Trollope and Brackett, plead guilty, and the third Hyde, escaped from arrest by tearing up bed clothes and letting himself out a third story window at Limerick.

Sarah T. Swett, of Bangor, now 67 years of age, has been bed ridden 36 years, and during that time has suffered almost every disease, contagious or epidemic, that has visit that city, including cholera. The Whig says that she appeared to be in the last stages of consumption 36 years.

The Machais Union says that S. S. Quimby, of Wesley has trapped nine bears within four weeks, seven old bears and two cubs.

Nathaniel Blaisdell, of Bath was found dead in his room last week, he had been dead at least two days when found. He was a person who acquired some notoriety as a great eater.

John Heald, of Madison, has planted twenty acres of potatoes this season. Mr. Ames, of Upton, and the farmers, all through the lake country, have planted unusually large fields of the same tuber, depending on the starch mills for a market. The usual price paid by the mills is 33 cents per bushel.

A child of Mr. McGinley, of West Houlton, two years old, was run over by a cow and killed last week.

Commodore Nutt and Minnie Warren were married in Connecticut on the 8th inst.

Henry J. Raymond, editor of the New York Times, died at his residence in New York on the 18th inst., very suddenly. He was seized with apoplexy at two o'clock in the morning and died at five o'clock.

## MARRIAGES

In Windham, June 1st., by Rev. Luther Wiswell, Lyman F. Mayberry, of Bangor and Miss Lydia F. Wentworth, of Windham.

In Gorham, June 19th, by Rev. H. B. Abbot, Wilson S. Rand and Miss Rosetta D. Tucker, both of Standish.

In West Gray, June 20th, by Rev. H. J. Bradbury, George Hunt and Miss Cynthia P. Smith, both of Gray.

In Gardnier, June 13th, by Rev. C. W. Morse, William A. Storer, of Hallowell, and Miss Mary E. Hodges, of Gardnier.

In Bristol, June 12th, by Rev. P. Rowell, Lewis Thorp and Miss Annie L. Seiders, also 16th, Robert Hanley and Joanna V. Sprowl, all of Bristol.

In Lewiston, June 10th, Collins B. Fenderson, and Georgia Jordan.

In this city, June 15th, Watson Freeman and Miss Julia A. Prentiss, both of Portland.

In this city, June 14th, Joseph F. Webber and Miss Mary Taylor, both of Portland.

In this city, June 15th, Almon Wight of Boston, and Miss Sarah E. Winslow, of Portland.

In this city, June 15th, Franklin H. Colby, and Helen Waters, daughter of the late S. J. Jordan, Esq., all of Portland.

In this city, June 15th, Theodore H. Johnson, of Pawtucket, R. I., and Miss Carrie S. Tukey, of Portland.

In this city, June 15th, Grenville M. Gross, and Miss Ellia G. Ross, both of Portland.

In this city, June 16, T. W. Sawyer and Maggie A. Lovejoy, both of Portland. [Oregon and California paper pleas copy.]

In this city, June 15th, Charles H. Stratton and Elizabeth C. Graves, both of Portland.

In Standish, June 15th, William H. Pray, of Saco and Miss Rosilla P. Marean, of Saco.

In Pownal June 10th, Elbridge G. Robinson and Miss Hattie W. Hunnewell, both of Auburn.

In Bath June 10th, James Murphy and Mrs. Sarah E. Poor.

In Paris, June 6th, Capt. Peter Hardy and Mrs. Marcilla Curtis.

In Hampden, June 7th, Brisley M. Jordan of Concord, N. H., and Miss Susie F. Hanes, of Hampden.

In Standish June 1st, Alfred S. Cousins of Baldwin and Miss Mary J. Cram, of Standish.

In Richmond, June 6th, Joseph F. Call and Victoria E. Cook.

In Skowhegan, June 3rd, William C. Poor, of Andover and Hattie A. Smith, of Skowhegan.

In Augusta, June 3rd, Jeremiah Kempton, and Annie E. Wright.

In Augusta, June 4th, George W. Dana and Lucy F. Follett, both of Gardiner.

In Readfield, May 31st, William Tufts, of Farmington, and Sophia D. Howes, Readfield.

In Gardiner, June 14th, John F. Winslow, of Westbrook and Annie E. Davis, of Gardiner.

## DEATHS

In Cumberland, June 8th, Annie G. daughter of Dr. F. S. and Olive M. Hall, aged 5 months and 7 days.

In Cape Elizabeth, June 13th Mrs. Ann M. Walls, aged 34.

In South Berwick, June 20th, Daniel Smith, aged 62 years, 8 months.

In Jefferson, May 9th, Mrs. Sarah M. Kennedy widow of the late Deacon John Kennedy, aged 86 years 8 months.

In this city, June 21, John M. Trefethen.

In this city, June 15th, Emma E. Noble, aged 14.

In this city, June 18th, Mrs. Mary Robinson, aged 81.

In this city, June 10th, Miss Sally Baker, aged 78.

In this city, June 27th, William H. Porter, aged 15.

In Topsham, June 11th, Anna M. Haley, aged 29.

In Harpswell, May 23, Miss Eliza Ellen Barnes, aged 20.

In Surry, June 14th, Capt. George W. Coggins, aged 36.

In Brewer, June 13th, Mrs. Clara Hodgdon, aged 41.

In Bangor, June 8th, Celia S. Montgomery, aged 17.

In New Gloucester, June 16th, Capt. Samuel True, aged 88.

In Bangor, June 17th, Mrs. Eliza L. Faulkner, aged 28.

In Livermore, May 8th, Mr. Jonathan Soule, aged 76.

In Kennebunkport, June 13th, Edwin Towne, aged 59.

In Anson, May 27th, Mrs. Rosilla Robbins, aged 67.

In Wiscasset, May 20, James McKeny, aged 62.

In Bangor, June 15th, Sarah T. Lovell, aged 69.

In Hudson, June 8th, Mr. Abram Colomy, aged 59.

In Oldtown, June 13th, Mrs. Clara A. Niles, aged 38.

In Ellsworth, June 4th, Zemna R. Smith, aged 15
In Waterville, June 6th, George H. Buck, aged 24
In Waterville, June 8th, Mrs. Ann D. Stevens, aged 39.
In Vassalboro, May 31, Benjamin Farnham, aged 70.
In Auburn, June 2nd, Harrison Goding, aged 28.
In Calais, May 27, Rodman V. Reed, aged 18.
In South Thomaston, June 6th, William Heard, aged 87.
In West Paris, June 5th, Mrs. Linnie H. Locke, aged 22.
In Bath June 11th, Vesta A. Blaisdell, aged 19.
In West Bath, June 13th, Mrs. Rachel Coombs.
In South Windham, June 17th, Nathan Cloudman, aged 68.
In North Fryeburg, June 4th, Simeon Charles, aged 81.
In Hallowell, June 8th, Emma Sherburne, aged 23.
In Readfield, June 6th, Franklin Bean, aged 78.
In Vienna, May 19th, Rufus H. Folsom, aged 60.

On the passage home from Boston, May 27th, suddenly Capt. Edward F. Gould, of Dresden, aged 57.

In Minneapolis, Minn., May 31st Gertrude H., only child of Alexander and Julia P. Tyler, aged 11 months.

# PORTLAND TRANSCRIPT

## July 3, 1869

Mr. William T. King, of Calais, has lost a fine young horse which he valued at $1000. Some internal injury is the cause of his death.

James Marden, a prominent and excellent citizen of Stockton, committed suicide on the 17th ult.

Joseph A. Kilbreth, of St. Albans, was fatally injured by the fall of a tree on the 21st ult.

The house of Mrs. Jacob Shaw, of Hancock, was burned about a fortnight ago.

E. L. Manter of Carmel, a painter fell 25 feet, on account of the breaking of his ladder and died on the 21st ult; the ladder was broken while he was "jumping" its top, so as to paint where the top had touched.

Isaac Babb, arrested for breaking into a store and flour mill at Saccarappa, confessed to other similar robberies in Gorham and this city; he implicated a young man named Edward Wallace, as a confederate.

Calvin Smith, who escaped from Thomaston State prison in 1867, was captured by detective Wormell, of Bethel, last week. He has four years to serve.

Edwin Mosher of New Vineyard, fell from the rafters of a new building, striking his head against a stone in the cellar and was severely but not fatally injured.

George Harris, Jr., a nephew of President Harris, has accepted the call of the High Street Congregational Church, at Auburn.

The house and out buildings of Mr. Bailey Donnel, at Bowdoinham, were burned on the 25th inst. Partly insured.

The dwelling and store owned by Mrs. Jane B. Sawyer, at Jonesport, were burned week before last.

J. D. Allan, of Dennysville, has bought and will run the mail route from Cherryfield to Eastport.

The remains of John Wilkes Booth, were buried with those of his family, at Baltimore last week.

Jeff Davis is at Paris in delicate health, and intends to spend the summer in Canada and the winter in Mississippi.

Henry T. Capen, a native of this city, but for many years a prosperous merchant in New York, died on the 17th ult., aged 65 years.

Brigham Young, in a recent sermon said he was often asked how many wives he had; that he had never though enough about it to stop and think, but would do so and set the matter at rest; supposed it was a dozen or fifteen that he took care of; and he added "I say, do not let any lady go to destruction."

Such instances as the following of the detection of criminals long after they suppose themselves safe should have a most salutary effect in deterring others from the commission of crimes. This most atrocious form of murder is fearfully prevalent, and several attempts recently made in this state, are fresh in the recollection of all.
The terrible accident at Carr's Rock in April, 1868, on the Erie Railroad, resulting in such wholesale slaughter, is yet fresh. From the fact that many thieves were on the ground who were known not to have been on the train, the great number of dead and wounded who were robbed, the subsequent finding of certain articles in the hands of suspected parties, convinced at least one man that the accident at Carr's Rock was not the result of a defective rail, but a deliberate attempt at murder for the purpose of plunder. Acting upon this theory and having placed at his disposal every possible facility by the managers of the road the matter has undergone a thorough investigation under the direction of one skilled in the detection of crime. Night and day for ten months suspected parties have been under the closest surveillance. Twelve men have been engaged in this work. At last on the 2nd June, sufficient evidence having accumulated to hope for a conviction, the suspected man, John Bowen by name was arrested, and confined in the county jail at Millford Pike County, Pa. After being confined fifteen days, Bowen confessed

his guilt. He is now awaiting the action of the grand jury, which meets at Milford in September.

Ex-Governor Seymour of New York, has lately recovered property amounting to the value of one million dollars, in a lawsuit.

C. B. Ives, the Connecticut sculptor has completed a plaster cast of the statue of Jonathan Trumbull, which is to be placed by the State of Connecticut in the capitol at Washington.

A woman, Mrs. Bell A. Mansfield, had been admitted to practice law in the courts of Iowa.

On the night of the 20th ult., burglars entered the store of Mr. Haynes, at Mason and got his safe out upon the platform, but a clerk happening along just then, and noticing the state of things went for help, and when he had returned the rascals had gone, taking only about $15 in all, which they found in a drawer.

## PORTLAND TRANSCRRIPT

### July 10, 1869

Mr. Sinclair, of Lisbon, attempted suicide quite deliberately a few days ago. He shot himself in the head with a pistol, before a mirror, in order to be sure of his aim. But he was surprised to find himself alive, the ball hitting his skull, and glancing upward. He was unwell, and despaired of recovery, and this was the cause of the rash and unsuccessful attempt. He received only a scalp wound.

Several aged people who are among the earliest settlers in Belmont have died recently. Mrs. Rachel Belcher, aged 92; Mrs. Sarah Elms, aged 83; Mr. Josiah Dunton, aged 67. They all lived in one school district and died within five days of each other.

Mr. Thomas of Gardiner, a constable of that city, and a truckman, had his horse's throat cut last week. The Mayor offers a reward of $500 for the detection of the miscreant who did it.

The house and store of T. J. Merchant of Damariscotta, was burned on the 27th ult. Loss $10,000 or more; no insurance.

William Russell, of Farmington, a young man 17 years of age, has been missing since last week.

The Lewiston Journal says that a veteran soldier was in that city last week, on his way to Island Pond, to see his family from which he had not heard for twelve years; he was covered with battle scars, have several bullets in him, and had some wounds still open.

David Bradley was found dead in his bed at the Oxford House, Fryeburgh, on the 28th ult., and an examination showed his death be the result of an internal hemorrhage.

Alexander Hughes, of Hodgdon, on the 25th ult, was upset with a load of clapboards, which fell upon him causing instant death.

F. W. Bickford escaped from Alfred jail last week and a reward is offered for his capture.

On Sunday last Mr. Lane of Readfield, went bathing with a little girl, and both were drowned. The same day a child of Isaac Perkins of East Winthrop was drowned.

Last Monday forenoon Mr. Arthur Buehrer, a young overseer at Long View Lunatic Asylum, Ohio went out with a company of the inmates to engage in some necessary work. About noon he was startled by one of the unfortunates calling to him, "Look Arthur, he is going to hit you!" Too late; he half turned when a pick axe, in the hands of one of the party, sank to the eye in his head, killing him instantly. The poor demented creatures wept when he fell, and secured the irresponsible perpetrator of the tragedy.

Ida Lewis, the Newport heroine, received a boat called the Rescue, from her admirers, last Saturday. Now she needs some one to help man it, unless she intends to ""paddle her own canoe" for life.

### MARRIAGES

In this city, June 29th William H. Sanborn and Georgie A. C. Crockett, both of Portland.

In this city, July 1st, George Curtis of Bowdoinham, and Mary A. Heidelbert, of Portland.

In this city, June 29th, Elvin C. Sweet and Miss Elvira Leighton, both of Westbrook.

In Boothbay, June 27th by Wilmot Lewis II, Esq., Alden B. Barter and Miss Mary J. Giles, both of Boothbay.

In Frankfort, June 24th, William P. Whitehouse, Esq., of Augusta and Eva Maria Treat, of Frankfort.

In Vienna, June 20th, Asa R. Moore and Miss Vill Ladd.

In South Windsor, June 16th, Moses J. Donnell of Pittston, and Ann E. Bryant, of W.

In Belgrade, June 6th , Hiram Ellis of Augusta and Ella R. Ellis of Belgrade.

In Bowdoinham, June 24th, Mulvy Partridge, of Woolwich and Susan W. Curtis, of Bowdoinham.

In Hebron, June 19th, Lafayette Starbird and Malvina J. Young.

In Hebron, June 20, Eleazer Snell of Buckfield and Cyrena Decoster of Hebron.

In Newry, June 20th George Crooker and Mary G. Smith.

In Lock Haven, Penn., June 24th, by the Rev. George W. Shinn, Alonzo M Millett and Miss Georgie Short, both of Portland.

In Brunswick, June 27th, George T. Pratt and Miss Jennie D. Noyes, both of Yarmouth.

In Hallowell, June 8th, Nathaniel L. Francis, of Rutland and Julia F. French of Chelsea.

In Hallowell, June 14th, George H. Woodard, of Gardiner, and May Lizzie Niles, of Hallowell.

In Kennebunkport, William W. Buzzell and Abba Plummer.

In Orono, June 24, David G. Stone and Mrs. Mary E. Drummond.

In Livermore Falls, June 5th Daniel C. Searls and Nancy A. Welch, both of Perkins Plantation.

In Livermore Falls, June 24th Horace A. Briggs, of Minot and Laura M. Nason, of Livermore Falls.

In Gardiner June 27th, Nathan P. Lyon, Esq., of Augusta and Mrs. Climena Mains, of Portland.

In Farmington, June 26th, George A. Stewart and Nellie A. Harvey, both of New Vineyard.

In Machias, June 12th, Martin Foss, of Marshfield and Evelyn C. Seavey, of Whitneyville.

In Rockland, June 27th, George Bond and Martha E. Huntley.

In Skowhegan, June 27th Samuel E. Smith and Joana F. Perkins, both of Cornville.

In Boston, June 27th, Philip W. Remick and Cora W. Niles, of Topham.

In Lewiston, June 26th, Albert P. Hardy, of Lewiston and Mary B. Ladd of Abbott.

In Lewiston, June 30th Chris G. Atkinson, of Oldtown, and Eliza E. Huntington, of Lewiston.

In Fayette, June 30th, Seth W. Johnson and Augusta C. Gile.

## DEATHS

In this city, June 30th, Dana L. son of Mary E. and A. L. Ames, aged 19 months.

In this city, June 29th, Mrs. Mary Smith, aged 37.

In South Paris, June 21, Mrs. Nancy P. Hill, aged 50.

In Poland, June 14th, Mrs. Wealthy Schellenger, aged 79.

In Farmington, June 19th, Nathan S. Davis, aged 69.

In East Wilton, June 22nd, Mrs. Sophia Burbank, aged 45.

In Saccarrappa, June 23 Mrs. Mary Goold, aged 28.

In Augusta, June 28th, Mrs. June C. Tibbets, aged 54.

In Pittston, June 18th, Enoch Hollis, aged 75.

In Bancroft, June 13th, Mrs. Mary Pomeroy, aged 90.

In Mechanic Falls, June 23rd, Mr. F. A. Duran, aged 33

In Poland, June 14th, Mrs. Filena A. Bradeen, aged 23.
In Eastport, June 20th, Elijah Harrington, aged 82.
In Sanford, June 21, Jacob Stanley, aged 84.
In Lyman, June 17th, Miss Bessie A. Trip, aged 27.
In Bath, June 24th, James Dolan, aged 48.
In South Berwick, June 7th, Ezra H. Meserve, aged 72.
In Temple, June 18, Phineas Parker, aged 65.
In Kingfield, June 11th, William Dagget, aged 61.
In Auburn, June 29th, Mrs. Betsey Davis, aged 78.
In Thomaston, June 25, Hon. Atwood Levensaler, aged 70.
In Bowdoin, June 23rd, Daniel Carter, aged 46.
In Thomaston, June 27th, Major David N. Piper, aged 73.
In Thomaston, June 19th, William Moody.
In Warren, June 26th, Job Spear aged 69.
In Bangor, July 1st, Charles E. Parker, aged 36.
In Clinton, June 13th, Jonas D. Burrill, Esq., aged 76.

## MEMORANDA

LAUNCHED.—At Thomaston, June 24th, from the yard of Simmons & Dunn, a three-masted schooner of 267 tons, named Georgie B. McFarlin to be commanded by Capt. Robert McFarlin, late of schooner Carrie Walker.

Schooner Nellie Tarbox, from Rockport, before reported at Wilmington, with a cargo on fire, has been scuttled and sunk at one of the wharves, the fire having broke out afresh.

Ship C. H. Soule, Callao, for Havre, arrived off Land's End 16th, and report June 8, lat 45 N, lon 22 W, passed an American barque painted black, abandoned and waterlogged.

Capt. William McGilvery of Searsport, will launch in a few days a brig of 250 tons to be commanded by Capt. Lowell Nichols. Another brig will be commenced as soon as the ways are clear.

Schooner Wanderer, of Rockland, recently ashore at Cape Henry, was launched from the ways at Norfolk, June 29th, having been new keel fitted and newly metaled. She has been purchased by a firm in Philadelphia for $10,000.

## PORTLAND TRANSCRIPT

### July 24, 1869

A Yarmouth correspondent sends us the following items, under date of July 14;

A son of Mr. Augustus True, aged about 6 years, fell from the wharf and was drowned on Monday afternoon last.

Mr. Thomas Bennett, who fell thirty feet from the bow stage of the ship Pacific, and was just able to work again, nearly cut off his left hand this morning, by having a scythe catch in a belt as he was holding it on a grind stone.

The Royals River Manufacturing Co., whose dam was carried away by ice last spring, have contracted with Mr. Greenfield Thompson to build the a permanent stone dam of their falls this season.

A boy named William Cooley, at Lewiston recently stole $55 from his father, and then hid himself, not making his appearance at night. A neighbor's house caught fire the next day, and the rogue could not resist the temptation to come out of his hiding place to see the conflagration, and the result was that he was caught, and will be sent to the Reform School; he has spent two dollars of the money.

Seth Morse has been appointed postmaster at Corinna, and Capt. Henry L. Wood, at Dexter.

Two little boys named Sawyer and Bradeen, were drowned at Limington on the 7th inst.

Mr. Alfred Nelson, of Eastport, has run ten miles in an hour on the Pembroke fair grounds. He attempted it at Eastport, but failed by three minutes, which the Sentinel explains by saying he was just "off a trot," and that the track was bad. The bystanders made up a purse of $25 for him.

The dwelling house and out buildings at Moderation Mills, in Hollis, owned by John F. Maddox of Alfred, and occupied by Rev. Daniel E. Maddox, was entirely destroyed by fire on Thursday week. The origin of the fire is unknown. Loss $2,500. Partially insured.

Rev. A. R. Abbott, of Rockland, who lately broke a limb, was recovering from the fracture, when he was seized with congestion to the lungs, and the Free Press of the 14th reports that he lies in critical condition.

Mrs. Catharine McDonald, of Augusta hanged herself on the 15th inst., from a beam in the cellar. She was 43 years old, and has been regarded as insane for the past year.

Dr. A. Pinkham, of Kendall's Mills, came near dying in a apoplectic fit on Sunday week, but was restored by letting blood.

George B. Blethen, of Unity dropped dead while at work on the highway, a few days ago.

From the Ellsworth *American* we learn that a Miss Tobey, in the employ of Mr. James W. Uran of Sullivan, fell down stairs Wednesday night of the 7th inst., and injured herself so badly that it is though she will not recover. Also that Mr. W. Hall of West Gouldsboro, fell dead in his house on Tuesday the 6th inst., and that a Miss Gould died instantly at Bar Harbor the 4th inst. She came to that place the day previous in the steamer Lewiston for the purpose for spending a few weeks at the island.

On Sunday, the 11th inst., occurred the fiftieth anniversary of the marriage of Mr. and Mrs. Isaac Richardson of Gorham.

A correspondent of the Rockland Gazette relates the adventures of William Grant son of the keeper of the Matinicus Rock lights, who was swamped in a sail boat on the 11th inst. As the boat filled, he attempted to throw out the ballast, but finding the boat was going down before this could be done, he dexterously capsized it, and thus threw out the ballast instantly. Over two hours he clung to the bottom of the boat, though washed off three times by the sea. The day was hazy and he could not be seen from the adjacent islands. Although the boat was heavy, flat-bottomed, 18 feet long, he concluded to make the attempt to right her, and by a quick movement succeeded. But he had lost sails, oars and rudder, and had nothing to bail with; he ripped off a piece of the head–board, and with it scooped out the water, though it filled a second time, during the tedious operation. Seeing the rudder floating at a distance he swam for it, and secured it, and then was able to keep the boat headed toward the land. He made a sail of some boards ripped off the craft, and at last reached Wooden Ball Island. These operation would be very difficult even under the most favorable circumstances, but it required remarkable smartness, coolness and skill to achieve them in the heavy sea then running.

## MARRIAGES

In Gray, July 10th, by Rev. E. Bean, Granville Waters, of Boston, and Miss L. Lizzie, daughter of William Libby, of Gray.

In Bridgton, June 23rd, by Rev. Mr. Fellows, Clayton D. Dresser and Miss Miranda Fogg, both of Bridgton.

In this city, July 5th, Charles H. Withinton and Miss Annie Wilson, both of Portland.

In this city, June 19th, E. W. Huston, of Falmouth and Miss A. L. Kilborn, of Cape Elizabeth.

In this city, July 19th, Charles F. Hall of Providence, R. I., and Miss Hattie W. Whitmarsh, of Pawtucket, R. I.

In Lewiston, July 4th, Stephen Gardner and Mrs. Adelaide E. Hall.

In Lewiston, July 13th, George F. Perkins and Miss Sylvia Davis.

In Augusta, July 1st, Edmund C. Folger and Carrie A. Weston.

In Augusta, June 26th, Frederic A. Wilson and Ella F. Moores.

In Brunswick, July 3rd, Levi Holbrook and Emma D. Paul, both of Harpswell.

In Brunswick, June 26th, George N. Kincaid and Irena C. Chase, both of Cornville.

In Newburyport, Mass., July 8th., E. S. Harrington, of Portland, and Miss Laura R. Hill, of Newburyport.

In Litchfield, Dexter W. Page, and Sarah J. Blanchard, both of W. Gardiner.

## DEATHS

In this city, July 8th, Mrs. Caroline Fessenden, of Brownfield, aged 33.

In this city, July 18th, William W. Woodbury, aged 59.

In Standish, July 13th, Miss Lydia Bavis, aged 75.

In Cornish, May 4th, John J. Haley, of Sebago, aged 53.

In Cornish, May 23rd, Samuel A. Bradley, aged 70.

In Cornish, May 26th, Edith only daughter of John and Josephine Bradley, aged 11 months.

In Fairfield, July 5th, Mrs. Lucy A., wife of Alfred Chase, aged 33.

In Gorham, April 28th, Richard H. Bean, aged 47 years, 7 months.

In Bath, July 11th, Christiana, daughter of Frederick Klippel, aged 9 months.
In Oxford, July 8th, Freeland Holmes, aged 61.
In Mechanic Falls July 11th, William H. Jose, aged 40.
In Gorham, July 13th, Mrs. Elizabeth Rounds, aged 60.
In Farmingdale, July 7th, William W. Allanes, aged 67.
In Rockland, July 1st, Ezekiel G. Dodge, aged 68.
In Brunswick, July 15th, Miss Caroline Weld, aged 73.
In Brunswick, July 15, Thomas Richardson, aged 69.
In Cape Elizabeth, July 20th, Mrs. Mary E., wife of Capt. A. M. Jordan, aged 40 years. Friends are invited to attend the funeral from his residence at 2 o'clock, p.m., Thursday, the 22nd.
In Springfield, Mass., July 17th John Collins, youngest son of J. W. Adams, formerly of Portland, aged 7 months.

## MEMORANDA

Barque Iddo Kimball, Delano, from Pensacola, for Montevideo, which put into Rio Janerio in distress, has repaired and proceeded 5th ult.

Schooner Clara Rank, at Wilmington from Boston, reports having been run into 1st inst., by a steamer, which stove in quarter and the house, and tore away main sail.

Schooner Abby H. Swasey, of Gloucester was totally wrecked on Half Moon Rock, 10th inst. She was valued at $6000, and insured for $4500, and $600 on outfit.

Schooner Republic, Boston for Wiscasset, which was run into 4th inst., and abandoned was towed into Gloucester 12th, by pilot boat Louisa Jane, after a week's labor, thus removing a dangerous obstacle to navigation, as both anchors were out.

Brig N. Stevens, at Washington from Bangor, reports having been struck by a terrific squall of Cape May and carried away mainmast.

Schooner, Eva L. Leonard, Bunker, while proceeding up North River, New York, on Friday afternoon, was struck by a squall and capsized. Crew Saved. The vessel was towed to pier No. 39.

Brig Charlotte, (of Bangor) Bowden, from New York, put into St. Thomas 19th ult., with loss of fore and main topmast. New spars were procured and she proceeded to Ponce for repairs. The weather was not rough at the time of the accident and breakage could no be accounted for.

Schooner James Henry, Oliver, Rockland, for New London, was in collision 10th inst., off West Chop, and had rail and plankshear broken and bulwarks stove.

## PORTLAND TRANSCRIPT

### July 31, 1869

Mr. David Batchelder, of Oak Hill, Cape Elizabeth, was seized, thrown down and so badly bitten on the arm by his stallion horse, on Tuesday evening of last week, that it became necessary to remove the arm at the shoulder joint, signs of mortification have set in, but little hope was entertained of his recovery. It took four men, with pitchforks, to get the horse off Mr. Batchelder. The same beast has previously killed one man and bitten off the thumb of another. It is about time he was knocked on the head.

On Monday week, at the steamer New York was leaving her wharf at Eastport, a passenger from St. John, named J. H. Cook, in attempting to leap on board struck the railing of the steamer and fell into the water, He was rescued by one of the crew, but was so severely injured that he died soon after.

Brigham Young has recently married again. His new bride is Miss Fallansbee, of Boston.

On Thursday week, a brake–man named Bryant on the grand trunk road, slipped under a freight train at Yarmouth, crushing his foot so that amputation was necessary. Bryant is a married man, 27 years old, and resides at Island Pond.

The Press learns that the report that Henrietta York has been pardoned is not true. The Executive Council favor a pardon but Governor Chamberlain has not yet acted upon the subject.

A jury at Fort Fairfield has found that a house of Henry Carter, burned a few weeks since, was set on fire by a Mrs. Warren, in the night.

On the 6th inst., the store of J. Hanscom & Son, in Milo Village, was destroyed by fire; stock saved. Loss $600; insured for $800.

A. Mr. Cummings, tutor to the son of the late Charles O. Rogers of Boston, temporarily stopping at Mattawamkeag, was shot in church at Winn, on Sunday last, by the accidental discharge of a pistol in his pocket, The pass passed through his shoulder, but the wound is not dangerous. The excitement in church was intense.

Henry Foss, of Machias, while fishing alone for lobsters on the 14th inst., fell across the gunwale of his boat injuring his stomach so that he died on the 16th. He was 35 years old, and leaves a widow and children.

Capt. John Merton, of Friendship, now eighty-seven years old, has not been sick a whole day for eight-one years, and never had a single tooth in his head, though he was always been able to eat his share of bread.

Mr. O. C. Frost, of Bethel, was thrown 30 feet down a bank, by the upsetting of a load of hay, on Friday week. He fell among rocks and stumps, but strange to say escaped with but a slight injury in the back.

It is said that Mr. George Peabody has completed his public donations. Let begging institutions take note, and allow the great philanthropist to pass the remainder of his days in peace.

At Knightsville, Cape Elizabeth, on Saturday week, William H., a son of John Harmon, and a boy named Victor Shannon, were thrown into the water by the upsetting of a raft on which they were floating. The Harmon boy, though lame, succeeded in seizing Shannon and pushing him on to the raft, from which he was rescued, but young Harmon, after this noble effort to save the life of another sank to the bottom, where his body was found clutching at the eel grass, as if to pull himself along. He was an amiable lad, 15 years old, and his death is a severe loss to his afflicted parents.

A house and barn belonging to Mr. William Arno, about three miles from Dexter Village, was struck by lightning, tearing up the floor and damaging the house about $100. Mrs. Arno had the sole torn from her shoe, but was not materially injured. A man who was unloading hay in the barn, and an ox attached to the cart, was knocked down but recovered from the shock.

Prof. Morse, of telegraph fame, fell down stairs at his residence in Poughkeepsie, last week, and broke one of his legs.

Miss Addie, only daughter of John Turner, and Flora, oldest daughter of Horatio G. Turner, both of Charlestown Mass., visiting in Auburn, Maine, and two sons of Rev. Mr. Libby of Auburn, were drowned in the lake at the latter place last Saturday afternoon. They were out in a row boat, which sunk. Two other persons in the boat escaped.

The Bangor Whig says that on Friday week, Thomas Clark, of Barkerville, having purchased a quantity of strychnine ostensibly to kill dogs with, after eating his dinner as usual, went into an adjoining room, and said he was going to take some medicine. In a short time he was taken in convulsions, and died very soon afterwards. He had undoubtedly poisoned himself, but no cause is assigned for the rash deed.

In a disturbance in Calais, Saturday night, John Lockwood of Dover, N. H., was injured so that he died Sunday morning.

## MARRIAGES

In this city, July 20th, Henry H. McDuffee and Miss Emma Keazer.

In Newport, R. I., July 13th Charles H. Boutwell, of Boston, and Miss Helen M. Abbott, of Portland.

In Kennebuck, July 15th, James H. Nason and Miss Fannie M. Barker.

In Hebron, July 16th, Samuel A. Bent and Miss Emily A. Bowman.

In Biddeford, July 11th, Albert P. Burleigh, of Boston and Miss Susie Staples of Biddeford.

In Bangor, July 17th, Horatio Blood and Miss Olive M. Dole.

In South Bridgton, July 11th, Alvah Johnson and Miss Mary A. Knapp.

In Pownal, July 18th, Standish B. Reed and Clara Cezeer.

In Lewiston, July 3rd, Samuel A. Cox, of Auburn and Miss Annett W. Briggs, of Lewiston.

In Rockland, July 18th, Jacob G. Ludwig and Mary Helen Kimball.

In Camden, June 30th, E. W. Thurlow and Sarah F. Healey.

In Rockport, July 17th, James E. Shibbles and Ella M. Fletcher, both of Camden.

## DEATHS

In this city, July 22nd, Charles B. Blake, son of Caleb Blake, of Turner, aged 24 years, 11 months, 13 days.

In Pownal, July 20th, Capt. Ephraim Penney, aged 74.

In Brunswick, July 15th, Mrs. Ruth Bailey, aged 77.
In Lewiston, July 13th, Mrs. Sarah Lincoln, aged 27
In Saco, July 13th, A. Mabel Stone, aged 18.
In Cape Elizabeth, July 21st, Geneva Chase, aged 22.
In Rockland, July 18th, Samuel Albee, aged 74.
In Wiscasset, July 11th, Benjamin Bladgon, aged 58.
In North Haven, June 27th Miss Olive Lindsey, aged 95
In North Berwick, July 2nd, Dr. Ivory H. Billings, aged 62.
In Sanford, July 15th, Howard Emery 24.
In Lovell, July 12th, Mrs. Joseph Bassett, aged 75.
In this city, July 24th, Frank Howard, only son of D. M. C. and C. K. Dunn, aged 4 years and 8 months.
In this city, July 25th, Alpheus Shaw, Esq., aged 85.
In Boston, July 22nd, of quick consumption, Samuel Chamberlain, aged 21 years, 7 months.
In Yarmouth, July 12th, Herman A., oldest son of Augustus W. and Harriet True, aged 5 years and 9 months.

## MEMORANDA

LAUNCHED-At Sullivan, 12th inst., from the yard of C. & W. H. Hall, a schooner of 93 tons, named Martha Weeks to be commanded by Capt. Charles Gilmore, of Belfast.

At Bucksport13th inst., from the yard of J. L. Buck, a ship of 1000 tons, built for parties in New York.

Brig Machias, Whitting, from New York for St. Mary's, Flordia, was run into 12th inst., while at anchor near Sandy Hook, and lost fore yard. She returned for repairs.

Schooner Augustine, Deer Isle, Capt. Scott, from Bangor, went ashore on Fawn Bar night of the 20th and filled. She got off next day and towed to East Boston where she will discharge and repair.

Brig A. F. Larrabee, from Bangor for New York, which capsized off Captain's Island, 16th , has been towed into Greenwich and righted and pumped out by the Coast Wrecking Co.

## PORTLAND TRANSCRIPT

### September 11, 1869

On the 1st inst., a construction train on the Bangor & Piscataquis Railroad, owing to a defective timber, broke through the bridge at Black Island, four miles above Oldtown, and the engine, tender and two cars fell into the river below. Conductor Woodard was instantly killed; Engineer Lander so badly scalded that he soon died, and seven or eight others were badly injured. Two laborers were supposed to be under the wreck, but they had run away. There were fifty persons on the train. The bridge was new, and had not been accepted from the contractors.

Gen. Sherman made a flying visit to our state last week. Slipping through Portland, by rail, he ran down to Bangor, where the people turned out at a short notice and escorted him to the Bangor House. He dined with Senator Hamlin, and the next day went to Augusta, where he entertained by Hon. J. G. Blaine. A serenade was given him and he spent an hour in receiving the people who pressed forward to take him by the hand.

Mrs. Thrasher of Ferry Village, Cape Elizabeth, awaking on Saturday night, saw the form of a man approaching her bed in the darkness. She screamed, he presented a pistol at her head, but her daughter running into the room and screaming too, the fellow took to his heels. He couldn't stand two feminine screams.

On Thursday week, as the Widow Verrill of Minot, with her two daughters was riding through Mechanic Falls, the horse became frightened, and they were thrown from the wagon. One daughter was thrown head forward against a stone wall, and immediately killed. The other occupants sustained severe injuries.

Jesse, only son of Joseph Hastin, of Kennebunk, climbed a tall tree on the 30th ult., to get a view of the location of the United States Engineers, and some hours after his body was found lifeless under the tree from which he had fallen. He was a promising boy, fifteen years old.

Buckfield has organized a Farmer's Club.

A lad named Leslie Austin, 15 years old sent from Androscoggin County to the State Reform School last April, having been found incorrigible, has been transferred to the State Prison at Thomaston, where he will remain two years.

Mrs. Robert Goddard, of Monmouth, was thrown from a carriage last week, and very severely injured.

Two years ago Joel Rand disappeared from his home in Alton. Last week two men came upon his remains in a thicket about a half mile from where he was last seen. They had not been disturbed, and he probably died the first night he was in the woods.

Bryant Hill, of West Parsonsfield, a youth of 18 or 19 years, attempting to jump to a gravel train at South Waterboro, on Monday fell beneath the wheel, which passed over him and cut off both of his legs. He died a few hours after the accident.

The body of Charles Goodwin was found floating down the river at North Limington, on the 19th ult. He was a river driver, and it is supposed he was drowned on the 14th, while attempting to ford the river above.

Rev. C. R. Moor, pastor of the Universalist Church in Augusta, while attending a funeral at Military Asylum, was thrown from his carriage and his leg broken.

Mr. Frank Rose, of Livermore Falls had the thumb and fore finger of his left hand cut off by a circular saw, on the 25th August.

Mr. Remembrance Leighton, of Biddeford, lost three fingers last week by having his left hand caught by a circular saw.

At Thomaston, on the 31st inst., a child of Mr. Bennett, two years old, and was drowned in a hogshead of water.

Mr. Robert Moors, of Pittston, died very suddenly on Monday, while sitting in his chair.

As a party were going from Norridgewock to Waterville, on Thursday week, the horses took fright and ran away. Mr. Cheney of Portland, and Miss Jackson, a teacher in the Eaton School, jumped out and escaped with some bruises. Mrs. H. F. Easton, wife of the Principal of Easton School, was thrown out and had her hip dislocated, and Mrs. Cutts, of New York, had her ankle so badly fractured that amputation of the foot had to be resorted to at once.

The Gardiner Reporter says that Mr. James H. Howland, mill wright of that city, had his skull fractured, on Wednesday week, by a piece of plank hurled against his forehead by a circular saw. Little hope was entertained by his recovery, but his symptoms are now more favorable.

## MARRIAGES

In this city, 1st inst., by Rev. George Tewksbury, James Nealey, Jr., of Bangor and Annie E. Lowell, of Portland.

Also, same inst., Stephen Harvey and Miss S. F. Nickerson, both of Portland.

In this city, Sept. 2nd, Thomas Bonner, of Eastport, and Gasgal A. Creg, Montreal.

In this city, Sept. 2., by Rev Father Murphy, Joseph F. Mackin, of Portland and Annie Koine, of New York.

In this city, Aug. 31st, by Rev. R. K. Harlow, George C. Whitehouse, of Boston and Jennie L. Wylies, of Portland.

In this city, Sept. 1, by Rev. James Pratt, D. D., Henry Sargent Trickery, and Sarah Emma, eldest daughter of D. H. Chandler, Esq., both of Portland.

In this city, Sept. 2, by Rev. Father Murphy, Thomas Bonner, of Eastport, and Georgie A. Cary, of Montreal.

In this city, August 30, by Rev. Mr. Southworth, John Stone and Ellen E. Hall; Sept. 4, by same Rev. Jothan S. Johnson, and Mrs. Eliza C. Johnson, of Portland.

## DEATHS

In this city, Aug.. 30., Alice, youngest daughter of Martin and Sarah I. Cuskley, aged 2 years and 9 months.

In this city, Sept. 2nd, Mrs. Harriet Woodman, aged 79.

In this city, Sept. 2nd, Mr. Daniel Plummer, aged 50.

In Westbrook, Sept. 1st., Mrs. Sibbel Wilson, aged 88.

In This city, Sept. 6th, Mr. Charles Elliott, aged 65.

In Falmouth 23rd ult, Ella S. daughter of Timothy and Eliza Merrill, aged 17 years and 8 months.

How solemn the hour; 'tis the triumph of death!
Disturb not the dying with tears;
The conflict has come, she has yielded her breath,
And closed up seventeen frail years.

Be still, troubled heart thy loss is her gain;
Oh! she is sweetly sleeping
Forever released from sighing and pain,
Reposing in angelic keeping.

How memory dwells on the past happy hours,
Of Ella, her childhood and home
When with her fond playmates she gathered the flowers,
Unconscious of the sorrow to come.

She dreamed not of lingering and wasting disease
That chills like the cold autumn day,
Which changes the foliage of beautiful trees,
And turns their green leaves to decay.

O! may she awake and be led by her lord
To drink the life giving river,
And witness the wonders of Eden restored,
And dwell with the ransomed forever.

In Bangor, Aug 20, of typhoid fever, Lyman F. Mayberry, formerly of Windham, aged 18 years and seven months.

Dearest Lyman, thou hast left us,
Here they loss we deeply feel,
But 'tis God that hath bereft us.
He can all our sorrows heal.

Peaceful be they silent slumber,
Peaceful in the grave so low.
Thou no more will join our number
Thou no more our songs shall know.

Darling Lyman, much we miss thee,
Much upon they name we dwell
Yet in Heaven, we hope to meet thee,
Where we ne'er shall say farewell.

In Cambridgeport, Mass., Aug. 31, Mrs. Elizabeth F. Cade, aged 71 years and 10 months.

Dearest mother, thou art sleeping;
They loved name we call in vain;
Never more they voice will greet us,
In the dear old home again.

Death's dark wave will bear us over
To that calm and peaceful shore
Where we all should be united,
And where parting comes no more.

There we know that thou art resting
On the loving Savior's breast
Father, Mother, Sister, Brother
All in Heaven, among the blest.

Blessed mother, may thy spirit
Hover o'ver our lonely home;
Come to comfort, guard and bless us,
Mother, leave us not along.

## MEMORANDA.

Schooner, L.T. Knight, of Camden from Philadelphia for Salem, with coal was fallen in with 29th ult, 60 miles from land; near Barnegat, abandoned in a leaky condition. She was worked into the Newport 30th, by a crew from the Fanny Blake. There are evidences of foul play in her abandonment, as three ¼ inch auger holes were found in the run, and captain and crew have not been heard from.

Schooner C.W. Dexter, Erskine, of and from Augusta, with lumber for Boston, struck on Sequin Ledge, 4th inst., and filled. She got off next day and taken to Bath for repairs.

Launched–At Yarmouth 6th, a first class double deck barge named the Charles Forbes–owned by B. Webster of Portland and others.

Also, from the yard of Stephen Sargent, at Westbrook, a first class brig named Mary Gibbs, to be commanded by Capt. Whittemore.

## PORTLAND TRANSCRIPT

### September 18, 1869

The Calais Advertiser says that a little son of Mr. W. C. Durgin, five years old, in attempting to cross the street, fell beneath a passing horse, which stepped on him in the region of the heart, killing him instantly.

Mrs. Elbridge Potter, of Brownfield was thrown from her carriage and instantly killed, at Tamworth, N. H., on the 1st.

On Wednesday week, a fire which caught in the stable destroyed the Emery Hotel, in Athens, and also the extensive stores of John Ware, Jr. The hotel was opened last December, and cost $20,000. The stores of Mr. Ware were more extensive that those of any other trader in the country. The Somerset Reporter learns that the hotel was insured for $19,000

The Patten Voice says that Mr. Zebedee Chandler of Washburn, is 77 years old and is the father of 18 children, 17 of whom are now living and have families. He has 40 living grand-children and great grand-children. He is still spry as most men are at thirty.

The thread spool manufactory of Messrs. Austin & Sanborn, in Weld, turn out, on an average, four hundred and fifty gross of spools per day, using four hundred cords of wood in the course of the year.

Shepard Bean of West Waterville, while working on a section of the track at Clinton Thursday week, was crushed between two cars so that he lived but a few hours.

Rev. R. Dunham, the big squashist, of Bryant's Pond, will only be able to produce a one hundred and thirty-five pounder this year. It has been a bad season for squash.

Cornelius Haley of Bangor was accidentally killed Thursday while cutting down a tree injured by the storm.

The death of Senator Fessenden makes it necessary for the Legislature elected on Monday to elect a Senator for his un-expired term.

Mrs. Esther McPheters, the first child born at Orono, died there on the 5th, aged 92.

Mrs. Harriet Beecher Stow has been quite ill at Stockbridge, Mass.

Mrs. Ruth Damon, pastor of the Universalist Church at Cavendish, Vt., has resigned and married another minister from Illinois. In this case woman's right to get married seems to interfere with her right to preach. To parody the words of an old song, we have here, "two single ministers rolled into one."

## MARRIAGES

In this city, Sept. 9th, by Rev. W. H. Fenn, George W. Cahoon, of Lyndon, Vt., and Miss Mary L. Bellows, of Portland.

In this city, Sept. 7th, John H. Hazen of Norway, and Lizzie S. Brown of Portland.

In this city, Sept 10th, Napoleon B. Stockbridge and Nettie Donnelly, both of Lewiston.

In this city, Sept 19th, Dr. B. F. Tasker, and Miss Fannie M. Foss, both of Kendall's Mills.

In Naples, Aug 27th, by D. H. Cole. Esq., Wallace D. Cole and Sarah M. Wright, both of Naples.

In Huntington, N. Y., Aug. 24th, Charles Curtis, A. M., formerly of Maine, and Miss Julia H. David, of Huntington.

In Westbrook, by Rev. J. O. Thompson, Samuel E. Turner and Clara M. Plaised, both of Westbrook.

In Denmark, Sept. 5th Alexander Boothby, of Portland, and Eliza A. Lowd.

In Lewiston, Sept 7th, Horace W. White, of Bowdoinham, and Andie M. Steward, of Lewiston.

In Auburn, Sept 8th, John W. May, Esq., and Hattie B. Wiggin.

In Hallowell, Aug 28, Orren Winter and Eveline Beals.

In Lewiston, Aug. 10th, Wesley W. Carlton, of Saco, and Rebecca F. Lane, of Lewiston.

In Livermore, Aug 19th, George Q. Gammon, and Betsey G. Bigelow.

In Bangor, Sept 1st., John F. Godfrey, and Abbie C. Bartlett.

In Bangor, Sept. 1, Nehemiah Kittredge and Marcia E. Low.

In Saco, Sept. 13th, William S. Noyes, of the York County Independent, and H. Imogen Whitten, both of Saco.

In Norway, Sept 4th, Abner L. Andrews of Otisfield and H. M. Maria Millet, of Norway.

## DEATHS

In this city, Sept. 7th, Margaret S. infant daughter of Dr. George and Clara H. French, aged 10 months.

In this city, Sept. 10th, Samuel N. Beale, aged 66,

In this city, Sept 6th, Gertrude R. , daughter of Charles A. and Media A. North, aged 9 months and 19 days.

In this city, Sept 8th., Mrs. Carroll Staples, aged 76.

In this city, Sept 11th., Charles E. Gray, aged 37.

In Baldwin, Sept 10th, Cyrus S. Snow, aged 66.

In Waldoboro, Aug. 25th, Nehemiah Leavitt, aged 52.

In Topsham, Sept 7th., Mrs. Mary T. Smith, aged 94.

In South Waterford, Sept. 1st., Hattie L., daughter of Charles and Harriet J. Young, aged 4 months and 15 days.

In Standish, Aug. 31st, Elizabeth A. Cressey, aged 38 years, 21 days.

In Saccarrappa, Sept., 4th, Solomon Conant, aged 67.

In Lewiston, Sept 4th, Kate Murphy, aged 17.

In Litchfield, Sept 5th., William Robinson, aged 72.

In East Winthrop, Sept. 3rd., Mrs. Nancy Blake, aged 82.

In Cape Elizabeth, Sept 6th William Snow, aged 20.

In Saco, Sept 1st., Anna E. Emery, aged 16.

In Saco, Sept 4th, Mrs. Laura F. Mason, aged 39.

In Auburn, Sept 6th, Mrs. Ellen H. Dewey, aged 27.

In Augusta, Aug. 11th, Sumner Haskell, aged 41.

## MEMORANDA

LAUNCHED-At Belfast 8th inst., from the yard of C. P. Carter & Co., a brig of 500 tons owned by R. Sibley and others, to be commanded by Capt. Colson, of Searport.

At Machias 6th inst., from the yard of J. M. Wiswell & Co., schooner of 200 tons, named the Gamma to be commanded by Capt. Urban Huntley, formerly of Tammany.

## PORTLAND TRANSCRIPT

### October 9, 1869

The Bangor Whig says that the oldest house in Bangor is on the corner of State and Howard Streets and is known as the Howard House. The land has been in the possession of the family 98 years. The birch tree under which the British ate their dinner, during the late war is directly opposite the house. Miss Fanny Howard, the owner of the house, has a spinning wheel over one hundred years old, also the oldest "grist mill", in Bangor, being an ancient mortar made by hollowing out a log, very primitive.

On Monday of last week, Robert Whitney of West Falmouth, fell some twenty feet in his barn, badly dislocating the left elbow joint, and fracturing the articulation surface of one of the bones. Dr. Hall of Cumberland reduced the dislocation and the fracture, and hopes to avert the much to be feared permanent stiffening of the joint.

Mr. David A. Davis, of Saco, at an early hour on Thursday week, went into his barn with a kerosene lamp to feed his horse. While on the mow the lamp exploded, kindling the hay, and barn, house and out buildings were totally destroyed. Insured for $1000.

On Monday of last week Cornelius Shaw of West Cumberland, fell from a load of hay, so severely fracturing the arm at the elbow that his attending surgeon, Dr. Hall is fearful that the use of the joint will be much impaired.

Rum drowned Bridget Simmons at the Head of the Tide, in Belfast last week.

The Calais Advertiser says that on the night of the 21st ult., the store of H. & P. Cullinen of that city, was entered and robbed of a new stock of goods, to the amount of $2,000. Some of the goods having been discovered in the barn of Mr. John Nichols. His son John and a companion named Eugene Leddy were arrested and the remainder of the goods were found hidden around the premises.

A deaf and dumb man named Finnegan was run over and killed on the track of the E. & N. A. railroad in Bangor, on Friday week. He was 45 years old and unmarried.

Mr. Jabez Bacon, the oldest man in Winthrop, aged ninety-three years appeared on the street last week with a horse twenty-five years old, a wagon forty-five years old, and a harness forty-eight years old. A gentleman engaged his attention while his photograph was surreptitiously taken.

Peter Riley, a laborer 32 years old, was killed on the line of the Portland & Ogdensburg Railroad in Westbrook last week, by a bank of earth caving in upon him while he was at work in a pit. He leaves a wife and three children near St. John, N. B.

Charles H. Wilson, merchant of Houlton had his leg broken recently by being thrown to the ground by a runaway horse.

The Passamaquoddy tribe of Indians have chose Lewey Beneuit to represent them in the next Legislature.

The Houlton Time give the particulars of a murder committed near the village of Munquart, N. B., two years ago. A discharged soldier named Holland disappeared at the time, and recently a body supposed to be his was found buried in the woods. Five men in the Parish of Kent and two in Aroostock has been arrested on suspicion of committing the murder.

A young man named White, said to belong to Vassalboro', at work for Lorenzo Gerald, of Benton, after retiring Friday night cut the muscles of his forearm to the bone, and when found life was nearly extinct. It is doubtful if he recovers.

Tobias Meader of Lewiston, was shot in the leg just outside the city a day or two since. Meader asked a lady he met on the road to ride, and as they drove along a jealous husband fired at them; so says the Lewiston Journal.

John M. Harding was attacked and beaten, while riding along the road, two miles out of Biddeford, on Wednesday night last, and the contents of his wagon stolen by two roughs.

Canton, in this state, has a lady Mrs. Winslow, 103 years old, who still knits very good stockings.

William Pendleton's house in Rockland was damaged by fire to the amount of $400, on Thursday week.

On Saturday, at South China, William G. Kingsbury was convicted of being a common seller, and the same evening the Second Baptist Church was set on fire and burned. Suspicion fell upon Kingsbury, and together with John Kitchen and L. B. Mitchell, he was arrested and committed to jail

On Monday week Mr. Eaton and Ivory Hilton, of Wells, went a fishing and in the afternoon the body of Eaton was found on the beach, near the boat; the other body was not found. The men leave families.

The smartest hunter in the vicinity of Deer Lodge City, Montana is Johnny Powell, a thirteen year old Snake Indian boy. When he goes for meat, meat comes. If it takes two or three days in the mountains alone, it's all the same to him.

In Boston last week, a wretch named Thomas Branning, beat his sober and industrious wife to death because she refused him money to buy rum.

The trial of Mrs. Harriet E. Parker for shooting Mrs. Baker, last June, on the Western Promenade, took place in the Superior Court last week, Judge Goddard presiding. The evidence showed that Mrs. Baker had ruined the happiness of Mrs. Parker by enticing her husband from her, that he abused and neglected her at a time when she most needed care and kindness, and that after suffering a miscarriage, and maddened by her wrongs, she sought the disturber of her peace, and fired four shots at her, inflicting dangerous wounds. A letter from Mrs. Baker to Parker was introduced, in which she urged him to fly with her to California, and to beware of that artful wife of his. The defense set up was insanity, and the prisoner's counsel, Judge Howard, went further, and took the extraordinary ground that even if she were sane at the time, she was justified in doing all she did, on the ground that she had a right to defend the chastity of her husband! County Attorney Webb, in reply, showed that the doctrine of self defense thus set up was a mockery not only of the law, but of common sense, and reason, since it would give every injured person a right to revenge their wrongs. The jury returned a verdict of "not guilty on account of insanity." The County Attorney thereupon moved that in accordance with the law, Mrs. Parker be committed to the Insane Asylum for treatment. This was resisted on the ground that she is not now insane, and Judge Goddard not only took this view of the case, but said no testimony had been presented which led him to believe that she had never been insane. This is undoubtedly the truth of the matter, and the verdict of the jury can only be explained on the ground that there are some offenses for which society still claims the right of private revenge. Mrs. Parker was discharged.

## MARRIAGES

In this city, Sept. 30th, Capt. George W. Mosher and Miss Roselvena Hatch, both of Portland.

In this city, Sept. 13th, George M. Cummings and Miss Lettie Stover, both of Portland.

In this city, Sept 25th, William W. Lucas, Esq., of Guilford, and Mrs. Martha S. Winslow, of New Gloucester.

In this city, October 3rd, Joseph F. Colley, and Miss Eunice A. Soule, both of Portland.

In Cape Elizabeth, Oct 2nd by Rev. B. F. Pritchard, Roscoe Libby and Nora Libby, both of Portland.

In Standish, Sept. 25th, Frank B. Smith and Georgia A. Waterman, both of Buxton.

In Standish, Sept 30th., Herman S. Whitney, of Gorham, and Villa A. Berry, of Standish.

In Lisbon, Franklin B. Toothaker of Richmond and Rebecca A. Bard, of Lisbon.

In Greenwood, Sept. 22nd., Howard D. Smith, of Oxford, and Mary C. Whitman, of Greenwood.

In Greenwood, Sept. 22nd, Harlow P. Staples of Auburn, and Sarah J. Whitman, of Greenwood.

In Bath, Sept. 30th, John Webster and Sarah L. Whitehouse.

In Standish, Sept. 30th, Herman S. Whitney of Gorham, and Miss Flavilla Berry of Standish.

In Dover, N. H., Sept. 15, by Rev. W. T. Chase, J. E. Jenks, Esq. of Portland and Nettie L. Perkins of Brunswick.

In Gray, Sept. 26th, by Rev. E. Bean, J. Henderson Cushing, of North Yarmouth, and Julia M. Nash, of Gray.

In Boston, Sept. 23rd., by Rev. D. Nickerson, of St. Paul's Church, Richard Osborne Dickson, of Bowmanville, Canada West and L. Maria Partridge, of Boston.

In Auburn Sept 28th, J. E. Burleigh of Holliston, Mass., and Miss Augusta M. Storab of Auburn.

In Dover, Sept 16th Edwin W. Graffam, of Portland and Mary E. Higgins of Gorham.

In Monmouth, Sept 26th, S. E. Bailey and Mary E. Tyler, both of Hallowell.

In Biddeford, Sept. 18th, James A. Fields of Falmouth and Ruth E. Lunt, of Biddeford.

In Augusta, Sept. 23rd, E. F. Plaisted, M. D., of Farmington and Frances S. Stanley, of Augusta.

In Bangor, Sept. 29th, Isaac M. Currier, and Helen A. Saunders.

In Oxford, Sept. 20th, Samuel A. Andrews of Otisfield and Clara E. Smith of Oxford.

## DEATHS

In this city, Sept. 3rd, Ida Louisa, youngest child of Charles H. and Sophia A. Rich, aged 5 years and 3 days.
In this city, Sept. 27th., John Deering, aged 85.
In this city, Sept. 28th, Mrs. Isabel W. Bailey.
In this city, Oct. 1st., Mrs. Jane B. Hatch, aged 81.
In Cape Elizabeth, Sept 22nd, Mrs. Amelia C. Cummings, aged 22.
In this city, Oct 3rd., Emery B. Richards, aged 23.
In Greenwood, Sept. 27th, Mrs. Mary Olive Whittle.
In Greenwood, Sept. 11th, Mrs. Irene Curtis.
In Cape Elizabeth, Oct 4th Ida L. Harford, aged 12.
In Augusta, Oct 2nd, Mrs. Carrie W. Frost, of Portland.
In Kennebunkport, Sept. 26th, Mrs. Ruth Cluff, aged 81.
In Biddeford, Sept. 26th., Hattie J. Hill, aged 24.
In Norridgewock, Sept. 27th., Mr. A. W. Freeman, aged 85.
In Buckfield, Sept. 29th, Mrs. Julia N. Long, aged 30.
In Skowhegan, Sept. 10th., Martha M. Gould, aged 30.
In Thomaston, Sept. 23, Mrs. Sarah Gilchrist, aged 89.
In Thomaston, Sept. 21st., John Butler, aged 65.
In North Yarmouth, Sept. 24th Beniah Titcomb.
In Bath, Sept. 26th, Hon George F. Patten, aged 82.
In Biddeford, Sept. 26th, Hattie J. Hill, aged 24.
In Buxton, Sept. 17th., Mrs. Hannah Ripley, aged 76.
In Saco, Sept. 26th, Mrs. Harriet J. Rounds, aged 23.
In Brunswick, Sept. 28th., Rose Skolfield, aged 20.

In Brunswick, Oct 1st., Mrs. Fannie L Cutter, aged 34.
In Harrington, Sept. 30th, Rev. Edward Brackett, aged 63.
In Kennebunkport, Sept. 23rd, William H. Cook, aged 47.
In Kennebunkport, Sept. 28th, Hillman B. McKenney, 23.
In Winthrop, Sept 28th, Dr. Robert Page, aged 47.
In Warren, Sept., 20th Harvey Blake, aged 70.
In Biddeford, Sept. 13th., Mrs. Eliza C. Allen, aged 38.

The bell tower at Pond Island Light Station was blown down in the late gale, and the bell injured. The ringing is discontinued until further notice.

LAUNCHED-At Thomaston 23rd., from the yard of S. Watts & Co., a ship of 1945 tons, not yet name, to be commanded by Capt. John Watts.

Also, from the yard of Stetson, Gerry & Co., a bark of 460 tons named the Alice J. Grace, to be commanded by Capt. George Smalley.

Also, at Damariscotta 23rd inst., from the yard of G. W. Lawrence, a barqe of 694 tons, named the John Justo, to be commanded by Capt. Bonhall.

## PORTLAND TRANSCRIPT

### October 30, 1869

Quite a severe earthquake shock was felt throughout the length of the state at about half past five o'clock on Friday morning of last week. People were awakened from deep sleep, beds rocked, bells rung, and there was a general oscillating sensation. The shock was of little less that a minute's duration, and was distinctly felt at Portland, Augusta, Gardiner, Belfast, Bangor, Eastport, and St. John, being very severe at the two latter places. At Belfast and Dexter a vivid glare suddenly appeared in the sky, and in some places a sound like a clap of thunder was heard. It isn't often we get a "shake" down east, so our people must be excused for making the most of a slight shock.

The Rockland Free Press states that during the recent tempest a bolt of lightning struck a small elm tree in the yard of Capt. M. R. Willey, only fifty or seventy-five feet from his dwelling. It broke a small limb in the top of the tree and then descended to the ground at its foot, not even scarring the bark on its trunk; when it struck the ground it threw up a furrow several feet in length, made a ditch a foot in depth, and threw turf over the fence into the middle of the street. Some of the roots of the tree were stripped of their bark.

Patrick Wing of Bath, was struck by the Kennebec train at Kendall's Mills on the 19th inst., and so badly injured that his recovery was considered doubtful.

George Barrett, of South China has been committed to jail to await his trial for willfully killing a horse belonging to Daniel Clark.

Mr. George E. Stewart, of Milltown, Calais, was drowned in Machias Mill Pond, at Eel River, a few days since.

Mr. Dearborn of Bangor, a wool buyer while riding between Clinton Gore and Hunter's Mills, last week, was beset by three men, who one after another got into his wagon and robbed him of $565. The rascals left his pocketbook and pistols in the wagon and made their escape.

Mr. William Hayes of Lewiston, lost one of the joints of a finger in the Androscoggin Mills on Friday week.

Marshal L. Kempton, son of Ezra Kempton, Esq., of Mount Vernon, while attempting to get upon a train of cars while in motion fell, the car wheels passing over his leg injuring it so severely as to require amputation.

Mrs. Betsy Robinson of Farmington, died from a apoplectic fit on the 6th inst.,

Joseph O' Brion, Esq. one of the wealthiest citizen of Machias died very suddenly on the 16th inst.

A house occupied by Frank Rust at Oak Hill, Swanville, was burned on the 15th inst.

The notorious James Brophy escaped from Auburn jail on Tuesday week, by jumping out of the door as the keeper entered his room and locking him in. Probably he is still at large.

Mr. Benjamin Pitts, of Waterboro' attempted suicide on Wednesday of last week by cutting his throat with a razor. No hopes are entertained of his recovery.

John Saunders of Whiting and Mrs. Cunningham, of Boston, were drowned on the 6th inst., by the upsetting of a boat at the falls between Dennyville and Whiting.

On the 18th inst., the youngest son of John M. Harding, of Saco, aged two years, met with a sad death by being scaled in a pot of boiling water which his mother had left for a few minutes. He lingered about thirty-six hours when death came to his relief.

## MARRIAGES

In this city, Oct 21st, George T. Means and Lucy A Dyer.

In this city, Oct. 21st, by Rev. W. H. Fenn, Joseph Webster of Lewiston and Mrs. Harriet N. Webster of Portland.

In this city, Oct. 20th, Joshua B. Irish, of Gorham and Miss Ellen A. Guptil.

In this city, Oct. 20th, John C. Small, and Mary S. Dresser, both of Portland.

In this city, Oct. 16th, Edwin Horr and Adaline Damrell, both of Portland.

In this city, Oct. 19th, Charles H. Mark and Mary A. Quint, both of Portland.

In this city, Oct. 21st, Harnden H. Jennings, of Farmington and Rhoda M. March, of Lynn, Mass.

In Washington, D. C., Oct. 20th at the residence of the bride's father, by Rev. Dr. Sunderland, Gen. Selden Connor, of Maine, and Miss Henrietta W. eldest daughter of John Bailey of Washington.

In South Natick, Mass., Oct 22nd., by Rev. E. C. Strong, Frank T. Bayley, of Gorham, and Julia M. Palmer, of Bath.

In Saccarappa, Oct 24th., by Rev. H. J. Bradbury, William A. Jordan, of Auburn, and Miss Verlinda McKenney of Saccarappa.

In this city, Oct. 16th., George F. Hanna and Miss Fannie E. Irwin, both of Portland.

In Brunswick, Oct. 16th., B. N. Adams of Boston and Miss F. G. Bradley, of Brunswick.

In Livermore Falls, Oct., 18th., Merritt C. Baldwin and Mrs. Abbie A. Richardson.

In Bar Harbor, Oct. 17th., George M. Young and Mrs. Adelaide S. Doyle, both of Eden.

In Cape Elizabeth, Oct. 21st., John B. Armstrong and Jennie M. Campbell, both of Cape Elizabeth.

In Portsmouth, N. H., Oct. 18th., C. P. Parker and Annie P. Holmes, both of Westbrook.

In New Orleans, Oct. 7th., Dr. S. Chapin Russell and Mrs. Martha W. Godfrey, both of New Orleans. [Press please copy.]

## DEATHS

In this city, Oct. 14th., William B. Robinson, aged 71.

In this city, Oct. 8th., Charles J. Dixon, aged 37.

In this city, Oct. 20th, Mrs. Sarah Carlton, of Hyde Park, Mass. aged 26.

In this city, Oct. 19th, Ophelia E., wife of E. D. Field, and daughter of Charles C. Crossman, aged 28 years, 2 months. [Corrected.]

In this city, Oct. 24th., Stephen Patten, Esq. aged 64.

In this city, Oct. 24th., Margaret J. Miller, aged 27.

In Gorham, Sept. 13th., Lizzie M. Clay, aged 6 years and 9 months, daughter of Joseph and Mary E. Clay.[Press please copy]

In Mexico, Oct 16th, Mrs. Phebe, widow of the late Jonathan Larrabee, of Hartford, formerly of Durham, 81.

In Westbrook, Sept. 26th., Charles C. H., son of David H. and Lucy A. Gowen, aged 7 months and 10 days.

In Westbrook, Oct. 3, Freddie E., son of Oliver H. and Hannah A. Leighton, aged 2 years and 10 days.

In Windham, Oct. 17th, Almira L. eldest daughter of William H. and Melvina D. Coffin of Raymond, aged 15 years.

In Limington, Oct. 6th of consumption, Frank O. Libby, aged 23 years, 4 months.

In Scarboro, Oct 14th, very suddenly Henry H., son of Woodbury and Abigail Libby, aged 28 years 5 months.

In West Gray, Oct. 14th, Mrs. Elvira, wife of Albert Pennell, aged 43 years, 1 month.

In Falmouth, Oct. 19th, Mary Ann Lunt, aged 46.

On Gorham, Oct. 5th, Caroline A. Cressey, aged 26.

In Otisfield, Oct. 16th., Eliphalet Wight, aged 68.

In Gray, Oct. 1st., Frankie W., only son of G. F. and L. A. Cobb, aged 3 years and 2 months.

> A flower more fair on earth ne'er bloomed
> Nor shone with brighter radiance here;
> Its sweetness was the light of home,
> And kindly nurtured was it there.
> Alas' life's chilly blast it ill could brook,
> And early drooped this bud of care,
> To us its bright leaves may withered look,
> It blossoms still 'neath Heaven's pure air.

In Cape Elizabeth, Oct 14th., Rosa youngest daughter of Charles and Rhoda Lindall, aged 16.

> Rosa went from earth and left us,
> Born away on angels wings;
> Now in heaven with holy spirits
> She sings the songs the ransomed sing.

In this city, Oct. 18th, Henry Ridgeway, son of William H. and Adaline A. Chase, aged 6 years, 3 months and 18 days.

> Child of promise! Who can bear
> Thus to see thee cold and still:
> Thou whose laugh rung on the air
> Like the music of the rill!
> Yet O, Father who shall dare
> Question thine Almighty will?

Child of promise! Who can bear
Dare we in our darkness dream
That they spirit standeth clear
In the heavenly noontide beam,
Watching o'er they loved ones here,
With thine eyes of tender gleam?

Child of promise! Child of hope
We shall miss thee on our road,
Bearing silently our load
Waiting, watching, down life's slope.
Until Heaven itself shall ope
And we see thee near our God.

Child of promise! Good and fair,
Beautiful in life were thou,
With the sunshine in they hair,
And the glad light on they brow;
Lovely here—what are thou there
Glorified forever now.

C. H.

## PORTLAND TRANSCRIPT

### November 6, 1869

Drs. Walker and Buxton, of Thomaston a short time since, performed a successful surgical operation for the removal of a cancer from the breast of Mrs. Mary A. Ripley of Appleton, The whole left breast was removed. The patient is doing well, and an early recovery is hoped for.

About a mile from Limerick village, Mr. Joshua Holland has an establishment for the manufacture of blankets. He has about completed a second building which will contain two full sets of machinery. He will employ one hundred hands, and his monthly pay roll will amount to about $2500.

Mr. Alphonso Deering, of Lewiston, on Friday week was attacked by a drunken man who tried to stab him with a dirk.

A son of Mr. Isaac Clough, about 17 years old, was upset in a sail boat, near Clam Cove, Camden, on Friday week and drowned.

Mr. Ephraim Stanley, father of Rufus Stanley of this city, a gentleman whose mind had been weakened by the infirmities of 76 years, wandered away from his home in Falmouth, on Thursday week, and after a long search by the neighbors, his body was found on Friday, in a pond, which he probably wandered in the dark.

Gov. Chamberlain has appointed Hon. Lot M. Morrill as U.S. Senator to fill the vacancy by the death of Senator Fessenden.

A small shingle saw mill at East Orrington, owned by David Savage II, was destroyed by fire on Saturday. Loss $2000. No insurance.

Mr. Benjamin Weston, of East Hebron was burned out on the night of the 26th ult., saving only his furniture.

A hundred Sioux Indians were burned to death in their camp on the Missouri River on the night of the 2nd ult., the prairie having been set on fire around them.

A house in Damariscotta, owned by William Flint and occupied by Sally Flint, and Joseph Gammons, was destroyed by fire on Monday week, the occupants barely escaping with their lives, some of them being nearly suffocated. They lost nearly all their goods. Partially insured.

Henry Emerson, of Castine, a deck hand on board steamer City of Richmond, fell overboard in attempting to go on board the steamer at Bangor, on Friday night and was drowned.

Lewis Phillips, a farmer fifty years of age residing in Auburn, was found dead in his bed on Thursday morning. Heart disease was the cause.

Oliver P. Stevens, has been appointed postmaster of Livermore.

Capt. Nathan Freeman and wife celebrated their Golden Wedding at their residence in West Bridgeton on the 28th ult., which was well attended by their children, grandchildren, relatives and friends, amounting to nearly one hundred persons; and the aged couple were the recipients of many useful present which were gratefully received. Rev. Jacob Bray, after a short and appropriate speech made by the bride, congratulated the aged couple by making some felicitous remarks, which were well received. A bountiful repast was provided for the occasion and a large, sumptuous loaf of wedding cake, furnished by their eldest son's wife, Mrs. Mary C. Freeman, of Lawrence, Mass, graced the festive board. Amid the conviviality it was proposed to send the editor of the Portland Transcript a generous slice of the cake with the donor's best respects.

Capt. Freeman and wife were years ago residents of Cape Elizabeth. He was then a shipmaster and sailed out of this port.

## MARRIAGES

In this city, Oct. 29th, by Rev. A. Dalton, Henry Frederic, and Margaret F. Counce, both of Portland.

In this city, Edwin J. Carruthers of Portland and Laura A. Dunton, of Hampden.

In this city, Oct. 29th, by Rev. Mr. Southworth, Adna T. Cushman of Auburn and Marcena Harding of Boston.

In this city, Oct. 30th, John A. Scott and Mary E. Deering, both of Portland.

In Raymond, Sept. 23rd, by A. B. Jordan, Esq., Mr. Oliver Brown and Miss Mary E. Watson, both of Gray.

In Greenwood, Oct 17th, Zachary T. Swan and Martha F. Yates.

In Turner, Oct, 17th, Charles S. Davis and Rose E. Harris, both of Auburn.

In North Auburn, Sept. 30th, W. H. H. Verrill, of August and Laura J. Russell.

In Lewiston, Oct. 26th, Gideon Cushman of Auburn, and Mrs. Susan Young of Lewiston.

## DEATHS

In this city, Oct. 30th, Benjamin C. Fuller, aged 48.

In this city, Oct. 31st, Capt. Joseph . White, aged 47.

In this city, Oct. 29th, Frank P. Woodbury, aged 22.

In this city, 29th, Miss Mary L. Wheeler, aged 73.

In this city, 29th, Mr. John McGowan, age 34.

In this city, Oct. 26th, Mrs. Marcia W. Hoyt, aged 33.

In this city, Oct. 29th, Eunice Shapleigh, aged 76.

In this city, Nov. 1st., George B. Clark, M. D. , aged 35.

In this city, Nov. 1st. Thomas Leonard Willis, aged 27.

In this city, Nov 1st., James Poole, aged 83.

In W. Gorham, Oct. 27th , Mrs. Mercy Topping, aged 84.

In Lewiston, Oct. 28th, Nettie B. daughter of George A. and Lotta B. Callahan, aged 1 years, 3 months.

In Brooklyn, N. Y., Oct. 27th, Josie H., youngest child of George and Elizabeth Sanborn, formerly of Portland.

In Cape Elizabeth, Oct 24th, Lydia P. Cameron, formerly of Southport, aged 26.

In East Auburn, Oct.. 26, Lewis Phillips, aged 50.

## PORTLAND JOURNAL

### November 13, 1869

The largest saw-mill in the world is at Orono, Me. It is four hundred and forty-feet long, sixty-six feet wide, has four gang-saws, five single saws, two circular saws, five lath machines, one shingle and one clapboard machine. It saws daily two hundred thousand feet of long lumber, two hundred thousand laths, ten thousand shingles and four thousand clapboards, and by requirement of law it burns up about one hundred and twenty cords of waste wood each day. It rents for $25,000 a years.

In Bangor, a butcher names Louis Reynolds was killing sheep by knocking them on the head with a hammer when, missing the animal, he brought the hammer with full force upon his leg just below the knee, breaking the bone short off.

Mr. John Griffin and wife of Stockton, celebrated their Golden Wedding on the 21st ult. Capt. William Clifford and wife of Searsport, were present, who were at the wedding fifty years ago.

The Lewiston Journal says that J. R. Pulsifer, Esq., of Poland, had his leg broken on Tuesday week, by the sudden starting of a team with which was drawing stumps.

On the 29th ult., Dellie, the only child of Augustine and Sarah Wyman, of Skowhegan was so badly burned that she lived only eleven hours.

The Farmington Chronicle gives an account of one Ward who, after stealing a horse and pung from John Crosby, of Avon, a buffalo robe from Benjamin Hunter of Strong, and a new harness from James Vining, escaped from his pursuers and started for Canada via Dixfield.

The Biddeford Journal says that there are four brothers, by name Samuel, Aaron, Philemon and John McKenney, living in Saco, whose united ages are 358, averaging about 90. Old Jenkins of Saco, will be 102 if he lives till January.

The following postmasters have been appointed in Maine; Harvey S. Crowell, at Winsor, Samuel Libby, at Orono; Andrew G. Berry at Smyrna.

On Tuesday week a house in Pittston, belonging to Amos Rollins, was burned together with it contents. Loss $2000, insured $600.

Fuller Dingley of Gardiner was severely bruised by the falling of his coal shed while he was fixing up the sluice way.

Mr. Henry Witham, of Waterville, as we learn from the Mail, had moved into a house which he had just brought and nearly paid for when, one day last week, it was burned to the ground with barn, shed and all their contents leaving his family stripped of everything save the clothes they stood in.

Two men named Williams and Libby broke out of Wiscasset jail on Thursday night of last week. Williams was arrested in South Gardiner on Saturday, and the officers were in hot pursuit of Libby.

Miss Molly Larrabee, who died in Lyman, on the 21st ult., in the 96 years, lived and died on the spot where she was born, and never was twenty-five miles from the home during her life time.

On the 2nd inst., the house of Capt. Jasper A. Roberts, in Winterport, was wholly destroyed by an incendiary fire. It was unoccupied.

Mr. Edward Cole, of Saco had his hand split nearly to the wrist by a circular saw on Saturday.

Gen Wool is very ill. He is 86 years old.

Miss Annie Cary, of Gorham, who for the past four years has been studying music in Europe, has made her appearance as a *prima donna* at Brussells, with immense success.

## MARRIAGES

In this city, Nov. 2nd, at St. Stephens Memorial Church of Bishop Burgess, by Rev. A Dalton, Mr. Joseph H. Short, and Miss Hattie A., daughter of S. R. Leavitt, Esq., both of Portland.

In this city, Nov. 8th, Rev. P. M. Hobson, of Standish and Martha Nevens of Gorham.

In this city, Nov. 3rd., by Rev. W. H. Fenn, Mr. Isaac Bushey of Richmond, Canada and Miss Lizzie A. Morrill of Danville, Canada.

In this city, Oct. 29th, William R. Simpson, of Gray and Sarah A. Dickinson, of Portland.

In this city, Oct. 30th, John A. Scott and Mary E. Deering, both of Portland.

In this city, Oct. 30th Edward Cobb and Lucy Robinson, both of Portland.

In Cape Elizabeth, Nov. 4th, by Rev. B. F. Pritchard, Daniel P. Graffam and Annie F. Scott, both of Cape Elizabeth.

In Lynn, Mass, Nov. 2nd, by Rev. A. H. Currier, Mr. Rodolph Greenwood and Addie Brancroft, both of Lynn.

## DEATHS

In this city, Nov. 8t., Jabez C. Woodman, Esq., aged 65.

In this city, Nov. 3rd, Mrs. Ellen O. Adams, aged 20.

In this city, Nov. 14th, James Poole, aged 83.

In this city, Nov 1st., John H. Burke, aged 45.

In this city Nov. 3rd, William E. Kimball, aged 64, and Susan A. Thorn, aged 17 years, 7 months, 5 days.

In Bridgton, Oct. 21st, Sarah Belle, daughter of Gardner B. and Sarah J. Boynton, aged 2 years 8 months.

In Windham, Nov. 4th, Hattie S. Rice, only daughter of Sawyer and Mary Rice, aged 15 years, 2 months.

In Scarboro', suddenly, at the residence of Samuel Durgin, Daniel J. Towne, of Saco, aged 37 years, 4 months 2 days.

In Saccarappa, Oct 29th, Jonas E. Butterfield, aged 29. He was bore his sickness with Christian calmness and patience, without murmur or complaint and at last fell asleep in the arms of his Saviour, no more to return to us but if we are good and true, we can go to him when Jesus comes to make up his jewels.

In this city, Oct. 20th Anna Eloise, only daughter of N. S. and Susan J. Fernald, aged 1 years 5 days.

Close the eyelids, close them gently;<br>
Sever one dear golden tress;<br>
Fold her icy hand all meekly<br>
Smooth the little snowy dress.

Farwell Annie, now the tear drops
Falleth for Alas! We know
Thou our fireside will be lonely
We shall miss our darling so.

When the evening shadows gather
We shall wait in vain to feel
Little arms all white and dimpled
Round our necks so softly steal.

Our wet cheeks will miss the pressure
Of sweet lips, so warm and red;
And our bosoms, Oh! How sadly
Miss that darling little head.

We'll not murmur, this is only
The clay dress our darling wore
God had robed her as an angel
She hath need of this no more.

Fold her hands; and o'er her pillow
Scatter flowers all pure and white
Kiss that marble brow and whisper
Annie, dear, goodnight, good night.

In Bridgton, Oct. 24th Willie Warren, child of Albert B. and Mary Frost Kilborn, aged 5 months and 26 days.

Go lovely babe, go to they rest
The Savior bids thee come,
Go join the ransomed and the blest
And leave this earthly home.

PORTLAND MAINE

November 20, 1869

The Reporter says that two houses in Gardiner, belonging to Mr. Eastman and Mrs. Moore-both families being absent-were broken into on Tuesday night, and robbed of bedding, silver ware and other goods. The articles were found on the premises of Alonzo Wakeman and Charles Kenniston, both offenders are now in jail.

Mrs. Abigail Kilgore, now ninety–four years of age, draws a pension as the widow of a Revolutionary soldier, and resides with her daughter in Dexter, who is also a widow and draws a pension on account of a son killed in the Rebellion.

William Tibbetts, of Litchfield, a lad of ten years, while attempting to place the belting on a grind stone, in a grist mill in Gardiner, on the 10th inst., was caught in the shaft and killed, he body being most horribly mangled.

Jacob Morrill, Esq. of Limerick has found, behind some boxes in his barn, the $300 for stealing which Alex Welch is now serving a term in the state prison. It was, no doubt secreted there by Welch.

Mr. Charles Sawtelle, of Bangor, fell from the roof of a two story house, headlong to the ground, a distance of thirty feet, yet strange, to say, escaped without any broken bones, though badly bruised.

A one story building in Dexter village, belonging to Dr. G. A. Haines was considerably damaged by fire on Thursday night of last week.

On Tuesday week a fatty tumor six inches in width was removed from the shoulder of William Emery, Esq., by Mr. Merrill of Madison.

The dwelling house of Capt. Jasper A. Roberts of Winthrop was burned on the 2nd.

The barn of Randall McCrillis of Palymyra, was burned on the 11 inst., together with 40 tons of hay, his crop of grain, 16 head of cattle, 2 horses and 2 hogs. The family were all at meeting, except an old lady. The main part of the house was also nearly destroyed. Only $300 in insurance.

A son of Mr. Hosea Ripley, of Bethel, aged 12 years, while amusing himself one day last week, by jumping from one platform of the cars to the other, while the train was in motion, near Walker Mills, fell between the cars, and the train passed over him, killing him instantly.

The wife of Capt. M. N. Folsom, of Bangor, who had just returned from the Insane Asylum at Augusta, supposed to be cured of insanity, attempted to commit suicide on Friday week by cutting her throat with a razor. It was thought the wound would prove fatal.

On Friday week the house and stable of Henry Williams, at Cape Elizabeth were entirely destroyed by fire; furniture saved in a damaged condition. Loss, $5000; insured for $3,600. The fire took from a defect in the kitchen chimney.

J. C. Locke, of Biddeford, his son Timothy H. Locke, his grand-daughter Mrs. Henry Moore, and the latter's children, are all living under the same roof.

Mr. Samuel Ober of Brooklin, dropped down dead on the road a fortnight since, while on his way to his daughters. His age was 96.

The Lewiston Journal says Mr. George Smouse of Waldoboro' has a hatchet that was used by an Indian in an attack made on the Dutch settlers in 1746. An Indian approached Mr. Smouse's grandfather and struck the hatchet through his skull, and for some unknown cause left in there where it was found by his neighbors, still sticking in his brain. The hatchet was been preserved in the family. It is an elegant instrument, and was probably owned by some chief.

In a mill at Orono, Friday week, Mr. Gilman W. Carr, a young man 23 years of age became entangled in the chain of the "rigger wheel," and his body revolved around the shaft seven times, the chain encircling him at each revolution, crushing his body terribly and causing death almost instantly.

Three of the rag pickers of New York are worth ten thousand dollars a piece.

William Brown, of Sanford, lost by an incendiary fire, on Thursday night of last week, his house, barn, a pair of oxen, three cows, one horse, one hog and all his farming tools, furniture, hay grain and other produce. Loss about $5000; insured for $1000.

Col. Alfred Johnson, a well known citizen of Belfast, died suddenly at the St. James Hotel, Boston on Sunday night, of lung disease. He was going south for his health. He was 44 years old.

Capt. John Walker, an old resident of Exeter, was found in his store, Wednesday week, in an unconscious state, having fallen from an upper story down the stairs. His skull was fractured.

The murderer Pike, in his speech from the gallows, lifted up a warning voice against intemperance, which had destroyed his life and periled his soul. He entreated those who deal in intoxicating drinks to stop that dreadful work.

A little son of Horace Chappel, of Biddeford, during the absence of the family from the room, set his clothes on fire with some matches, and was so terribly burned that he died the next day.

Joseph Millay, of Camden, lost his right arm by the premature discharge of a blast in a lime rock quarry, at Blackington's Corner, on Tuesday week.

The dwelling house of Harvey Campbell, of Bowdoinham, was burned on Wednesday week; furniture saved. Loss, $1000.

## MARRIAGES

In this city, Nov. 11th., at State Street Church, by Rev. W. H. Fenn, Horace Anderson and Miss Mary E. Wood,

In this city, Nov 3rd., George Fogg of Boston and Mrs. Martha Plummer, of Portland.

In this city, Nov. 9th., at the First Parish Church, by Rev. B. H. Bailey, Frank W. Newhall and Ellen S. Green, both of Portland.

In this city, Nov. 9th, at the by Rev. W. H. Fenn, Robinson Williams and Emma E. W. Chenery, all of Portland.

In this city, Nov. 14th, Alvin H. Jacobs, and Nellie E. Sturgis, both of Portland.

In Farmington, Nov. 7th, Lendall C. Marston and Miranda North, both of Farmington.

In South Paris, Nov. 6th, Winfield S. Partridge and Miss Frank (sic) R. Barrows, both of Norway.

In Dover, N. H. Oct. 20th, Albert O. Phillips, of Alton Bay and Miss Mary S. Frost, of Portland.

South Montville, Oct. 24th Elijah Gay and Flora A. Cushman.

In Biddeford, Nov. 6th Charles W. Wells, and Mary A. Butler, both of Biddeford.

In Lewiston, Nov. 6th, Joseph H. Dunton, and Georgiana Austin.

In Augusta, Nov. 1st., John W. Sands, of Lewiston and Helen M. Rollins, of Augusta.

## DEATHS

In this city, Nov. 3rd, Capt. Thomas C. Stevens, aged 74.

In this city, Nov. 1st, Miss. Sarah A. Reed, age 27

In this city, Nov. 14th Emma H. Melvin, aged 17.

In Bridgetown Center, Oct 19th, John A. son of W. H. and Susan T. Thorne, aged 17 years, 7 months and 5 days.

In Alfred, Nov. 6th of typhoid fever, John H. Trafton, aged 60 years, 1 month, 25 days.

In Dresden, Nov 4th., Jasper 8, son of Thomas G. and Mary S. White aged 18 years, 10 months, 4 days. [Rockland Free Press please copy.]

In Bridgton, April 25th Mrs. Hannah, widow of the late Deacon Benjamin Larrabee, aged 73.

In Falmouth, Nov. 8th, Ethelyn infant daughter of Jason H. and Emma F. Winslow, aged 4 months, and 8 days.

In Naples 4th, Mrs. Martha H., wife of Kingman Perham, aged 38 years, 2 months 8 days.

In Cape Elizabeth, Nov 1st, Mary H. Richards, aged 20.

In East Auburn, Nov. 4th, Benjamin Bradbury, aged 57.

In Cape Elizabeth, Nov. 12th, Mrs. Sarah A. Ingraham, aged 74.

In this city, Nov. 10th, Annie E. infant daughter of C. D. and E. A. Thomas, aged 13 weeks.

This lovely bud so bright so fair,
Laid in the dust so low.
Did bloom to show how bright a flower
Could blossom here below.

PORTLAND TRANSCRIPT

December 4, 1869

Capt. William Williams, of Kennebunk, who was superintending the building of a new ship there, on Monday week, fell unobserved from the lower deck to the lower hold, a distance of fourteen feet, breaking his neck. When found the body was cold, and must have been lying there two hours. Capt. Williams was about fifty-five years old, a native of England, and during a residence of fifteen years in Kennebunk, had won the esteem of all by his genial, honest and upright deportment. He leaves a invalid wife.

In West Falmouth, on Tuesday week, Hannah Elliot, a woman of unsound mind while attempting to do some ironing in the absence of her sister, set fire to her dress and rushed into the road enveloped in flames. Before the neighbors could get to her, her flesh was literally baked and came off her in great flakes. She lingered in great agony for about an hour, when death put an end to her suffering. She was between forty and fifty years of age.

During the storm of the 20th ult., the schooner P. S. Linsey went ashore on Stag Island, and is nearly a total wreck. She was owned by Capt. Linsey of Wells, and Kendall & Jordan of Biddeford, Six men from the Pool rescued the crew. Loss about $7000.

An ovarian tumor weighting fifty-six pounds was successfully taken from Miss S. Patten, of Burnham, on the 16th inst., and one weighing twenty pounds was removed from Mrs. George Hammons, of Sweden on the 20th inst.

The mills known as the "Rattle Trap Mills" in Surry, owned by P. S. and J. A. Milliken, were burned Saturday night, Nov. 14th. Partially insured.

Victor Morriette, of Biddeford, as he went down a flight of steps for water, slipped and fell into the river and was drowned.

Another death from venturing on the ice. A little son of George H. Baker, of Lincoln was drowned on Tuesday, while skating.

A boy named Ruel Sanborn, was drowned at Jackson Village on the 17th ult.

The convicts in the state prison had a turkey dinner on Thanksgiving day, and were allowed three hours recreation in one of the large shops, which they spent in talking, singing, jumping and dancing, without restraint, all behaving with propriety. It took 232 turkeys to feed the 177 convicts.

Mr. Benjamin Gilbreth, who recently died at Kendall's Mills at the age of 88 years was a soldier in the war of 1812, was with Scott at Lundy's Lane and rescued that General when he fell into the Niagara River, by plunging in after him, for which he was made a sergeant.

In Bangor, on Friday morning John Hennessy got into a quarrel, while intoxicated with Michael Mogan, night porter of the Penobscot Exchange, and was shot by him so that he now lies in a critical condition. Mogan was arrested

The dwelling house, barns and out houses of Mr. Horatio Hill, in Baring N. B., with nearly all their contents were destroyed by a fire a short time since. Loss about $8000. Insured for $3000.

Hugh Twoney, of Milford, fell off the railroad bridge at that place, on Monday week and was drowned.

Mr. John Ripley of Bath, aged 96 is the oldest man in that town. He is able to walk to church.

Rev. Dr. Parker, pastor of the First Congregational Society in Gorham, celebrated his Silver Wedding on Friday week, on which occasion the members of the society presented him and his wife with a silver tea service, and a purse of money amounting to $200.

Dr. Livingstone is promised a title and a pension if he returns to England.

Near Nashville, Tenn., on Sunday week one Joe Barton returning home and finding his wife and three children all in bed together, cut the throats of the whole of them, and then fled. The murder was not discovered until ten o'clock the next forenoon.

The wife of the Rev. J. C. Adams of Falmouth, fell from a chair while hanging up a bird cage on Monday week, and broke one of the bones of her right leg. Mrs. Adams has been particularly unfortunate, having broken her left leg and wrist some time since.

Gen. Neal Dow has been conducting a very satisfactory temperance campaign in Massachusetts.

Hon. Hannibal Hamlin lectured on Agriculture at Levant on Monday week, and at the close a Farmer's Club was formed.

Clara Barton is making a tour of Switzerland and visiting the family of a young Swiss soldier whom she nursed during the war. Clara is delighted with Europe and has been everywhere well received.

## MARRIAGES

In this city, Nov. 21st., by Rev. G. A. Tewksbury, Isaac H. Brown of Portland, and Harriet N. Penfield of Gorham.

In this city, Nov. 25th, Alphonzo C. Jones and Abbie Ella Knight, both of Portland.

In this city Nov. 23rd, Henry Gerrard, U. S. Navy, and Lydia J. Blanchard, both of Portland.

In this city, Nov. 25th, William H. Cluff, of Portland and Jennie S. Whitten, of Saco.

In this city, Nov. 24th, Thomas F. Fuller, of Boston and Eugenia A. Moody, of Portland.

In Dover, N. H., Nov. 25th, at the Kimball House, David F. Smith and Nellie P. Chick, both of Portland.

In Leeds, Nov. 24th, C. H. Farley and Elsie H. Wing, both of Portland.

In Bowdoinham, Nov. 16th, Augustus M. Stilphen of Pittston, and Nancy L. Williams of Bowdoinham.

In Gray, Nov. 22nd, by Rev. A. B. Lovewell, Cephas W. Low and Eliza B. Whitten, both of North Yarmouth.

In Naples, Nov. 18th, by D. H. Cole, Esq., George D. Staples and Lydia E. Jordan, both of Raymond.

In Newport, R. I., Nov. 18th, by Rev. A. Dalton assisted by Rev. William Leverett, Capt. Francis H. Bailey and Susan Jordan, both of Westbrook.

In Saco, Nov. 25th, Roger Edwards, of Brooklyn, N. Y., and Mary S. Coolbroth of Saco.

In East Boston, Nov. 9th, Joseph Arnold of Detroit, Michigan and Carrie B. Bailey of East Boston.

In Dover, N. H., by Rev. I. D. Steward, A. M. Demerit of Strafford, N. H., and Martha L. Maxwell, of Norridgewock, Me.

In Wells, Nov 25th, by Rev. J. W. Sawyer, Oliver Stevens, of Wells and Maggie Render of Warrenville, N. J.

In Gorham, by Rev. C. C. Parker, D. D. Almon Littlefield of Standish, and Annie M. Blake of Gorham.

## DEATHS

In this city, Nov. 24th, Jane W. Strong, aged 71.

In this city, Nov. 24th, Peter Daly, aged 23.

In Dayton, Mrs. Betsey Mayberry, relict of Richard Mayberry, late of Gorham, Me.

In Amherst, Oct. 16th, Dr. A. Backus, aged 37.

In Cape Elizabeth, Nov. 24th, William Ricker, aged 58.

In Norway, Nov. 17th, Evi F., son of Steven H, and Mary A. Needham, aged 21 years and 13 days.

In Loda, Ill., of quick consumption, Nathaniel Rideout, late of Portland, aged 49.

## PORTLAND TRANSCRIPT

### December 11, 1869

Mr. G. W. Seavers, for many years the foreman of the manufacturing department in the firm of A. C. Denison & Co., of Mechanic Falls, is about to leave them to go into business with his brother in New York. Mr. A. T. Denison, son of A. C. Denison will take his place.

The late Col. Alfred W. Johnson, of Belfast, Me., gave Rev. Cazneau Palfrey, D. D., $200 per annum during his life; after his death the money is to be paid to his wife, after her death the same sum is to be yearly paid to his daughters or to the survivors of them.

The ceremonies of opening the European and North American Railroad from St. John to the state line, took place last week. A dinner was served and congratulatory speeches indulged in. Traffic trains begin to run regularly at once.

Mrs. Betsey Tobie, who died in New Gloucester on Sunday week, was 101 years and 5 months old. She retained her faculties well to the last says the Lewiston Journal.

Jacob Terrill, of Northport, committed suicide on Saturday week, by cutting his throat, while in a fit of temporary insanity. He was fifty years old.

Messrs. Morrills & Farrar of Buckfield have driven nearly 600 head of cattle to Brighton this season.

The book store of T. M. Varney, and the dry goods store of R. S. Ambrose, in Lewiston was destroyed by fire on Friday morning of last week, and sad to relate, Mr. M. D. Chaplin, a young lawyer was burned to death in his bed. He was probably suffocated by the smoke, and next morning his charred remains—one arm gone, most of both legs, the top of the skull and the abdomen, burned off—were found in the ruins of the building. He was about 30 years old, a native of Bridgton, unmarried, but said to be engaged to a daughter of William D. Little, Esq., of this city.

The house in Cape Elizabeth known as the "Lake Hill House," on the Ocean House Road, owned and occupied by Mr. A. M. Dinsmore, was discovered to be on fire as the family were seated at dinner, on Friday week, and was rapidly consumed, scarcely anything being saved. The property was valued at about $5000 without estimating the loss in the furniture, hay and etc.

Mr. Perez Chanzey of Trenton, aged 67 was found dead at the door of his dwelling house, on Sunday week. He was living alone and it is supposed his death was caused by bleeding at the lungs.

On Friday week a son of Watson D. Bean, aged fifteen years and a son of Henry Dougherty, aged thirteen, was drowned at Passadumkeag while skating.

An affecting incident occurred at the funeral of the late Francis E. Webb, who was buried with Masonic honors at Winthrop. Just before the body was removed from the house to the church, a little daughter of the deceased, Annie Dwight, came to the open casket of her father, which was covered with flowers, and on which stood the baptismal fond, and there in the presence of the "living and the dead", was consecrated to God in holy baptism.

Two more young men drowned while skating, Noah Ames at Locke's Mills, 21st ult., and Webster Reed, at Augusta on Saturday last. Who is prepared to be the next victim?

Daniel D. Blaisdell, of Dedham, fell from a scaffold in his barn on the 13th ult., and struck on a thrashing machine, receiving mortal injuries.

Mrs. Jonas Bisbee, while riding down a steep hill at North Paris on Sunday week had her leg broken by a kick from the horse.

One Major McCurdy, of Cardington, Ohio deliberately shot his own son dead because he took the part of his step-mother, the Major's third wife, to whom he was not faithful.

A correspondent informs us that Mr. George Warren of North Parsonsfield, on stepping to his door a few evenings since was suddenly surprised by a large owl lighting upon him and lacerating his arm quite severely. But the grave stranger anticipating trouble retreated a short distance, when Mr. Warren, who is plucky, and not easily frightened, seized his gun and brought the midnight marauder to the ground. He was of the largest size, his wings when extended measuring four feet in length.

Miss Delia Williams, of Gardiner, who the Reporter says, has been a great sufferer from disease of the knee joint, had the thigh amputated on Wednesday week, and one of her fingers was also taken off at the same time.

## MARRIAGES

In this city, Nov. 24th, by Rev. George A. Tewksbury, George A. Thompson, and Emma D. Meserve, both of Portland.

In this city, Nov. 30th, Charles F. Holden, and Emeline Farrington, both of Portland.

In this city, Nov. 30th, Lewis C. Breed, and Allie Butler, both of Portland.

In this city, Nov. 25th, C. T. Tuero and Annie S. Fernald, both of Portland.

In this city, John Deering and Rosa C. Davis, both of Portland.

In Buxton, Nov. 18th, by Rev. C. H. Gates, Frank J. Leavitt, and Jennie O. Lewis, both of B.

## DEATHS

In this city, Dec. 2nd., John Curtis, 69.

In Atkinson, Nov. 11th, Benjamin Cilley, son of D. C. and Abigail Cilley, aged 24 years and 7 months.

In New Gloucester, Nov. 28th, Mrs. Betsey Fickett, widow of Richard Tobie, aged 101.

In Washington, Oct. 6th, of typhoid fever, Caroline, wife of William Lenfest and daughter of Rev. Micha Howard, aged 57.

May 8th, Frank Walton, son of Henry D. and Callie Noyes, of Providence, R. I., aged 9 months,

November 15th after a long sickness, James Lenfest, aged 42 years, 7 months [Mass. papers please copy.]

In Nevada City, Cal., Sept. 7th, of typhoid fever, Randall P. Alby, aged 31.

In Liberty, Oct 14th, of consumption, Hiram Turner, aged 56.

PORTLAND TRANSCRIPT

December 18, 1869

On Saturday evening schooner Mary Ellen, Gilpatrick, Saco from Boston loaded with hard pine lumber, went ashore on the spits; hoisting signals of distress, an extra crew came to her assistance, and while the captain went into the port for a steamer to take his vessel off, his trunk was rifled of all its contents, including $185 in cash.

The Light House Board has given notice that the fixed white lights, varied by flashes every thirty seconds, will be exhibited after the 15th inst. from light stations on and near the center of Docket's or Sennot's Island, in the St. Croix River, opposite Red Beach.

The Anson Advocate informed us that the dwelling house, barn and out-buildings belonging to Mr. Roland Luce of Lexington, were totally destroyed by fire Sunday afternoon. Nothing was saved but the live stock in the barn.

Seth Kelly was instantly killed on Tuesday week by the bursting of a large grindstone in Hubbard, Blake & Co.'s, scythe ship at West Waterville. He leaves a wife and a child.

Two trains on the Maine Central collided Thursday week, on the railroad bridge over the Androscoggin River, which nearly resulted in throwing them from the bridge.

Mr. William Wagner of Rockland, on Thursday week, was knocked down and robbed of seventeen dollars while on the way to visit his daughter.

Miss Ada Penley of Biddeford, caught her hand in some machinery in one of the mills, crushing two fingers of the right hand severely.

Mr. James Rogers of Bath, had his right hand badly crushed, by being caught between the body and the tongue of his cart.

Mr. Benjamin Davis, of West Poland was nearly drowned on Saturday week. Mr. Davis attempting to cross on the ice, which had frozen over only the night before broke through. By holding on to the floating ice, and with the assistance of two men who heard his cry, he was rescued.

Edgar Emery and James Avery have been sent to jail to await trial for breaking and robbing the store of Mr. Lougee on Factory Island, Saco, of about $100 worth of property on Thursday week.

Sloop Stephen Orr, Capt. Herriman, of Cape Elizabeth, loaded with stone was run into and sunk during the storm of Monday last, in Seal Harbor. No lives lost.

Capt. George T. Harper, of Mount Desert, master of barque Armenia, died Oct. 9th, at Gibraltar, of inflammation of the lungs.

Mr. I. P. Longfellow, of Machias, narrowly escaped drowning a few days since while skating.

Mr. David Crane of Warren, on his seventy-second birthday, walked from Warren to China Village, a distance of thirty-six miles inside of eleven hours, including dinner, which is pretty good for a man his age. Mr. Crane takes and reads the Transcript, which partly accounts for his youthful vigor. F. L.

The Bangor Whig says that Mr. George Cole, of Oldtown, lost his pocket book containing $1400, while jumping from the cars at the E. & N. A. R. .R. depot Saturday night. Monday morning he came to Bangor and found his pocket book buried in the snow near the track.

A little daughter of Isaac Martin, of Kittery, six years old was burned to death the other day by her clothes catching at a fire built by her little brothers in the woods near their home.

A schooner called the E. M Sawyer, 131 tons burthen, was launched on the 4th inst., from the yard of D. J. Sawyer, Jonesport. Capt. D. D. Kelly is to command her.

### MARRIAGES

In this city, Dec. 7th, by Rev. A. Dalton, assisted by Rev. J. Pratt, D. D., Rev. D. A. Easton, of Danbury, Conn., and Miss Margaret Ellen, youngest daughter of S. T. Corser, Esq. of Portland.

In this city, Dec. 8th, by Rev. W. H. Fenn, T. Coleman Allen and Helen Bailey, both of Portland

In this city, Dec. 7th, Rev. Charles A. Hayden and Carrie Ormsby, both of Farmington.

In this city, Dec. 7th, Hiriam Libby and Jennie E. Moody, both of Limington.

In this city Dec. 9th, Charles F. Libby and Alice Bradbury.

In this city, Nov. 18th, at the residence of the bride's father, No. 241 Congress Street, Rev. Mr. Root, John S. Green and Mary F. J. Colburn.

In this city, Dec. 5th, by J. M. Edwards, Esq. Thomas G. Kimball of Albany and Margaret Good of Portland.

In Saccarappa, Dec. 12th, by Rev. H. J. Bradbury, Isaiah D. Leighton of Falmouth and Abbie M. Bodge of Windham.

In Westbrook, Nov. 15th by Rev. George A. Tewksbury. John M. Jordan and Mrs. Fannie Jordan, both of Westbrook.

In Standish, Nov 2nd, William Thompson and Mrs. Maria Dow, both of Portland.

In North Bridgton, by Rev. E. F. Borchers, William Carsley of Harrison, and M. Augusta Smith, of North Bridgton.

In Wiscassett, Dec. 7th, by Rev. John N. Marsh, A. P. Thompson, of Minneapolis, Minn., and Rose Alley, of Wiscassett.

In Wells, Dec. 5th, by Rev. J. W. Sawyer, George N. Dockham and Mary E. Furbish, both of Wells.

## DEATHS

In this city, Dec. 8th, M. E. Black, aged 13.

In this city, Dec. 7th, William Causer, aged 40.

In this city, Dec. 9th, Miss Ann Davis.

In this city, Dec. 7th, Mrs. Jane Elizabeth Doyle, 25.

In this city, Dec. 13th, James W. Westwood, aged 47. Funeral Wednesday, P. M., at 1 o'clock from No. 33 St. John St. Friends invited.

In this city, Dec. 11th., Mrs. Emily Emery, formerly of Halifax, N. B., aged 83.

In New Durham, N, H, Cassie M. daughter of Eli P. and Sarah L. Watkins, aged 1 year, 7 months, 29 days.

In Chelsea, Mass. Dec. 12th, of quick consumption, Mrs. Jennie P, wife of William M. Libbey, formerly of Portland and daughter of Deacon R. Rideout of Cumberland Center, aged 38 years, 4 months, Funeral Thursday p. m. at 2 o'clock from her father's residence.

In Winthrop Dec. 9th, Benjamin Robbins, aged 80 years, 3 months.

In Denmark, Sept. 19th, Mrs. Priscilla, wife of Cyrus Ingalls, aged 60 years, 9 months, 8 days. [Wis. Paper please copy.]
In Palermo, Samuel H. Worthing, Esq., aged 74 years.
In Hingham, Mass., Nov. 27th, Mrs. Bertha Hobart, 86.

At a special meeting of the Portland Mechanic Blues the following resolutions of respect to the memory of their late comrade William Paine, who was at one time an active, and at the time of his death an honorary member of the Company, were presented and by them adopted.

*Whereas* it has pleased our Heavenly Father to remove from our midst the kind husband and father, the genial companion, the true friend and esteemed citizen William Paine, therefore,

*Resolved*, that as an active and a honorary member of our Company, we ever found him ready and eager to aid us in all our enterprises.

*Resolved* That we will ever cherish him memory sacredly, believing that to him we are largely indebted for the success which has always attended our organization.

*Resolved* That we sympathize deeply with the afflicted family and relatives of the deceased knowing, as we do, that the loss to them is a severe one.

*Resolved* That the business community have ever found in him a true champion, an honest man and by his death their ranks have lost a worthy member.

*Resolved* That a copy of these resolutions be sent to the family of the deceased, and

*Resolved* further, that the resolution be presented to the company now present as a token of our respect for the memory of the departed, with the request that they be entered upon the records of the company.

*Resolved* That a copy of these resolutions be furnished the papers of our city for publication.

Capt. George W. Parker, Lieut., C. J. Pennell, Lieut. E W. Lovitt, Lieut. R. T. Wescott, Private, S. K. Knight, *Committee on Resolutions.*

## PORTLAND TRANSCRIPT.

### December 25, 1869

Two young men calling themselves Frank and Lester Foster, were arrested Monday week by Marshall Hill and Officer Pratt of Biddeford, for setting fire to the small depot at the Camp Grounds at Kennebunk, and also for obtaining money of Thomas Simpson of Biddeford under false pretenses as we learn from the Democrat.

Dr. George W. Martin, assisted by Drs. Freeze and Kinsman, of Augusta, a short time since removed a fibrous tumor from the eye of Mrs. Seth Gay.

Richmond has a Tom Thumb specimen. A son of Mr. Joseph Totman is eight years old, stands 21 ½ inches in his shoes and weighs 24 pounds.

Mr. Peter C. Smith and wife of Bethel, celebrated their Golden Wedding on the 2nd inst.

A drunken spree among laborers on the Portland & Ogdensburg Railroad in Standish, on Friday week, resulted in the killing of John Macarty by William Logan. Macarty was about 23 years old. Logan came from New Brunswick, is 37 years old, and has a wife, who was mixed up in the melee; one of the drunken laborers named Berrigan, taking indecent liberties with her for which Logan gave him a drubbing, and next day got into a fight with McCarty with the above fatal result.

Gen. Tilton has been prosecuting rum sellers who sell to the inmates of the Military Asylum at Togus. These men are so depraved as to settle near the Asylum for the express purpose of selling liquor to the soldiers.

Dr. Alfred Hall, the venerable and well known physician of Alfred, died on Saturday at the age of eighty-three. He had been a resident of the town sixty years.

A child of Capt. McFarland of Belfast, lost an eye last week from the thrust of a red hot poker in the hands of another child.

Walter S. Waterhouse, of East Machias has been pardoned out of the state prison, because his is dying of consumption.

A boy in Peterboro, N. H. finding an old gun barrel placed it in the stove. The result was his mother lost her hand.

The house of John Dolan, Washington Street, was badly damaged by fire on Saturday night, and the family turned out only with a change of clothing.

A boy six years old was killed by a snow ball in New York the other day.

Mr. Benjamin Marble, who attempted suicide on Sunday week died a few days after, perfectly conscious, but with no recollection of the attempt as he wondered what made his neck so sore.

During the drenching rain of Thursday night Officer Barbour found a woman lying on the sidewalk dead drunk with an empty bottle by her side.

## MARRIAGES

In this city, Nov. 14th , in the Bethel Church, by Rev. Mr. Southworth, Joseph Briggs of Paris and Carrie A. Coffin of Portland.

In this city, Dec. 10th, John L. Bardish and Mrs. Susan C. True of Portland.

In this city, Dec. 19th A. F. Emery and Mary E. Smith, both of Portland.

In Standish, Nov. 1st, by Esq. Thompson, Rufus Roberts and Ernestine Chick. [The happy couple had the rare fortune to go through the marriage ceremony twice in one week, there being some informality about the first performance.]

In Vassalboro', Dec. 9th, W. E. S. Whitman, (editor of the Bath Times) and Clare E. Abbott of Vassalboro'.

In Cape Elizabeth, Dec. 15th by Rev. B. F. Pritchard, William Hamilton and Julia M. Frickett, both of Cape Elizabeth.

In Buckfield, Nov. 27th by Rev. Mr. Benson E. H. Watson, of Cape Elizabeth and Persis M. Hutchinson, of Buckfield.

In Falmouth, Nov. 17th, by Rev. J. C. Adams, S. H. Thompson of Woburn, Mass., and Julia Merrill of Falmouth.

In Baldwin, Dec. 12th, John Hern and Maria L. Berry, both of Sebago.

In Portsmouth, N. H., Dec. 9th, Ira G. Page and Mary McLane both of Portland.

## DEATHS

In this city, Dec. 13th, Mrs. Clara Rugg, aged 50.
In this city, Dec. 13th, George Chamberlain, aged 31
In this city, Dec. 13th, Rufus Beale, aged 71.
In this city, Dec, 15th, Henry Gallison, Jr. aged 32.
In this city, Dec. 15th, Henry Merrill, aged 82.
In this city, Dec. 15th, Benjamin Merrill, aged 65.
In this city, Dec. 18th, Helen M. W. Quincy, aged 63.
In Sidney, Dec. 10th Climena Webber, wife of Daniel R. Townsend, aged 34.
In Yarmouth, Nov. 26th., Willie E., only child of W. H. and Phebe E. Marston, aged 5 months.

PORTLAND TRANSCPIRT

January 22, 1870

Margaret Ann Thompson, from the Provinces, was found frozen to death, near the railroad crossing at Morrill's Corner on Monday. She started for Portland on Friday in the extreme cold; a bottle of whiskey and a bottle of rum, found under her, explained the cause of the sad affair.

The death of Meltiah Lawrence, of Gardiner, aged 99 years and 4 months, brings out a family record remarkable for it longevity. His mother was 97, his sister over 100, and two brothers respectively 97 and 94.

Leander Pinkham, of Hallowell, is under arrest at Framingham, Mass. for setting fire to a house in which a lady was burned to death.

It is a notable fact that one fourth of the convicts in our state prison are boys under 21, and the average age all under 29. There are now 174 convicts, the largest number ever in the prison; 84 were committed in 1869 none of whom were from either Aroostook, Franklin, Lincoln or Oxford counties.

A valuable trotting mare belonging to Mr. McLaughton, of Bangor had the shaft of a sleigh plunged into her breast eight inches, while at the top of her speed last week. The shaft was withdrawn and she is doing well.

The jury was unable to agree on the case of Micah W. Norton, of New Portland, who complain of being tarred and feathered by his neighbors in June 1866.

Henry Baker and wife, in the S. J. Court, have recovered damages from the city for injuries received by having been thrown from their wagon on a heap of paving stones in the middle of the street, to the amount of $3300; the defense was assumed by the Portland Water Company, who have filed exceptions.

Judge Goddard, last week sentenced O' Harra, the entry thief to five years in the state prison; Robert Graffam, for stealing a yoke of oxen, got two years, Edwin Clark and George Pierce for compound larceny, got respectively five and ten years and Charles Shelden and John Campbell, as common thieves got respectively five and four years.

Two nephews of Gen. Gideon Pillow were shot and killed near Leighton, North Alabama, a few night ago, by a band of masked men, who escaped.

## MARRIAGES

In this city, Jan. 11th, Walter Douglass and Mary Ann Steele, both of Portland.

In this city, Jan. 13th, Charles O. Kennard and Josephine B. Lovejoy.

In this city, Jan. 13th, Charles A. Charleton and Ellen J. Sargent, both of Portland.

In this city, Jan. 16th, George M. Coburn of Portland and Mary E. Pollister, of Westbrook.

In Beloit, Wis., George L. Purington, of Chicago, Ill., formerly of Portland and Seppie K. Blodgett, of Beloit.

In Lewiston, Jan. 13th, Henry C. Litchfield and Hattie L. Rollins.

In North Yarmouth, George H. B. Stevens and Hanna H. Williams, both of Standish.

In Saccarappa, Jan. 15th, by Rev. E. P. Thwing, George Stackpole, of Gorham and Abbie E. Brackett, of Saccarrappa.

In Saccarrappa, Jan. 16th, by Rev. H. J. Bradbury, Elbridge G. Bailey, of Westbrook and Emma Hartford of Hiram.

In Cumberland, Jan 12th, by Rev. E. S. Jordan, Louville H. Merrill, of the firm Sweeter and Merrill, of Portland, and Mary E., daughter of Capt. Charles Wyman of Cumberland.

In Pownal, Jan. 13th, Edward P. Griffin, of Freeport, and Mary A. Hayes of Portland.

At Edes Falls, Jan. 15th, by Rev. Mr. Andrews, Robert Edes, Esq., and Ellen M. only daughter of A. F. Wright.

In Sauk Centre, Minn., Dec. 24th, Capt. ------- Oakford and Nellie A. daughter of the late Dr. Reuel of Fryeburg, Me.

In Lewis, Dec. 30th, Deacon Charles A. Howland of Webster and Lydia H. Jordan, of Lisbon.

In Lewiston, Jan. 4th., James O. Carr and Miss Etta M. Ames.

## DEATHS

In this city, Jan. 12th, Mrs. Catharine, widow of Maurice O'Connell, St. John, N. B. aged 61.

In this city, Jan 12th of typhoid fever, Frank W. Newhall, aged 22.

In this city Jan 14th, Mrs. Ella S. Blake, aged 21
In this city Jan 15, Mrs. Abbie Sawyer, aged 32.
In Brunswick, Jan. 10th, Rachel Totman, aged 78.
In Brunswick, Dec. 23rd , Mrs. Huldah Cleaves, aged 70
In Sumner, Dec. 13th Mrs. Margaret Jordan, aged 52.
In North Lovell, Dec. 31st, Lucy, wife of Joseph Kilgore aged 71 years and 7 months.
In Gray, Jan 9th, Mrs. Susan Higgins, aged 63.
In Limerick, Jan. 1st., Mrs. Sarah S. Plaisted, aged 73.
In Milton, Dec. 5th., Mrs. Nancy Taylor, aged 82.
In New Vineyard, Mrs. Mary Winslow, aged 82.
In Friendship, Dec. 16th, Mr. John Studley, aged 85.
In Orrington, Dec. 20th, Rev. Heman Nickerson, aged 72.
In Yarmouth, Jan.12th, Ezekiel Merrill, aged 74.
In Boston, Jan. 10th, William Scott of Falmouth, aged 66.
In Bucksport, Jan. 11th, Capt. John Pierce, aged 72.
At Topsham, Jan 10th Mrs. Phebe Brimigeon, aged 77.
At Kendall's Mills Jane, 28th, Keziah Whitney, aged 57.
In Gardiner, Jan. 8th, Meltiah Lawrence, aged 90.
In Sidney, Dec. 20th, Deacon James Smiley, aged 80
In Skowhegan, Jane 9th, Sarah Neil, aged 89.
In Scarboro, Dec. 14th, Carrie W. Libby, aged 22.

In North Conway, Jan 9th, George A. son of Lorenzo and Susan A. Lamb, aged 2 year and 7 months.

> Great the pain, though brief the measure
> Of the life that now is o'er
> Now in heaven in ceaseless pleasure
> He will dwell forevermore.

## PORTLAND TRANSCRPIT

### January 29, 1870

Jeremiah Quimby, of Boothbay, who lost his life in the shipwreck of the schooner Mary, had the presence of mind to secure the identification of his remains, by writing his address on a bit of paper, which he wrapped in birch bark, tied with twine and stuffed oakum over it in his pocket. He took a similar precaution to secure his watch and chain.

Mr. Nutter of Castine, froze to death in attempting to cross the river from Brooksville on the 13th inst. He lost his way in the storm.

J. A. Hasty, postmaster and trader at Waterborough had absconded after obtaining thousands of dollars by forging the names of substantial citizens to notes, and raising the wind at the banks in Biddeford and Saco.

Isaac Bigford and Isaac Verrill, two young men of Tremont, upset their boat and were drowned while out gunning last week.

There is intense excitement throughout Franklin County in the matter of the killing of John S. Tolman by constable John Fletcher. The friends of the deceased claim that the homicide was entirely unnecessary , while Flecther claims that the act was in self-defense. Fletcher has recognized in the sum of $5000 to answer at the Supreme Court on the first Monday of March.

Revel, the Negro Senator from Mississippi is a graduate at Oberlain College and was educated for the Methodist ministry. He is forty years of age, gentlemanly in appearance and of a dark complexion, and is said to possess more that average ability.

Virginia, at last takes her place again as a state in the Union.

### MARRIAGES

In this city, Jan. 19th, by Rev. A. Dalton, James F. Smith and Celestia H. Richardson, both of Portland.

In this city, Jan. 20th, Emmons Chapman and Cleora F. Coolidge, both of Portland.

In this city, Jan. 16th, Lionel Brackett of Westbrook, and Adrianna F. Sherman of Edgcomb.

In Cape Elizabeth, Jan. 2nd by Rev. Mr. Atkinson, William H. Lindsey and Hattie Ricker both of Cape Elizabeth.

In South Berwick, Dec. 31st., by Rev. Z. S. Knight, Frank Knight and Clara J. Johnson, both on North Berwick.

In Windham, Jan. 20th, by Rev. L. Wiswall, William Wescott, and Hattie A. Gray, both of Standish.

In Portland, N. H., Jan, 20th, William B. Bibber and Josephine Mason of Portland.

In Lewiston, Jan. 15th Alfred J. Moore and Jennie E. Hoyt.

In Buckfield, Dec. 25th, Samuel Record of Lewiston and Clementine Turner, of Buckfield.

In Biddeford, Jan 9th., William A. Roberts, of Waterboro and Henrietta Mcdonald, of Biddeford.

In Belfast, Jan 2nd, Fred M. Sherman and Margaret J. Murphy.

In Yarmouth, Jan 19th Stillman Sawyer and Hattie D. Bates, both of Yarmouth.

In Yarmouth, Jane 20, Alvah S. Pickering of Portland and Estella L. Lord, N. Y.

In Augusta, Jan 11th, Charles F. Stone and Fannie R. Howard.

In Sanford, Jan 2nd, Joseph Ridley and Mary A. E. Lord.

In Bath, Jan. 18th, Samuel H. Colesworthy, Jr., of Portland and Nellie Lee, of Bath.

## DEATHS

In this city, Jan 21st, of typhoid fever, Stephen Swett, aged 58

In this city, Jan 23., Sadie F. Hervey, aged 23.

In Gray, Jan 4th, Mrs. Olive, wife of David Huston, aged 66 years, 5 months. [City papers please copy.]

In Saco, Jan 3rd, Mrs. Mary J. wife of the late Elisha Wadleigh, aged 39.

In S. Freeport, Jan. 20th Gershom Bliss, aged 44.

In Tremont, Jan 2nd, Samuel Lurver, aged 76.

In Searsport, Jan . 9th, Vienna H. Warren, aged 76.

In Gorham, Jan. 19th Mrs. Matilda Prince, daughter of the late Stephen Waite, of this city.

In Hollis, Jan. 15th, Mrs. Susan Foss, aged 66.

In Fayette, Jan 9th., Mrs. Emma B. Fitch, aged 36

In Turner, Dec. 30th., Mrs. Lorinda Harlow, aged 32.

In Standish, Jan. 2nd (?) Rev. James Weston, aged 78.

In Hartford, Jan. 3rd, Ephraim Russell, aged 64.

In Warren, Dec. 6th, Robert Montgomery, aged 86.
In Saco, Jan 11th, John F. Seavey, aged 22.
In East Hampden, Jan. 15th Mrs. Hiram Proutey, aged 73.
In Ellsworth, Jan. 10th N. T. Cunningham, aged 42.
In Lewiston, Jan, 17th, Charles E. Fogg. Aged 27.
In Waterford, Jan 18th, Stephen T. Proctor, aged 68 years, 2 months and 6 days. Of seven children, their ages ranging from 59 to 77, this is the first death.

In this city, Jane 17th, Eddie F., only child of Capt. J. P. and Martha B. Grace, aged 2 years and 8 months.
His little life was brief but beautiful.
[ Eastern papers please copy.]


## MEMORANDA

Schooner Mary W. Hupper, at Savannah 10th from New York reports on the 9th, while coming to anchor outside Tybee, the 1st officer, Mr. Hupper of Maine, in loosening the anchor was pitched overboard and drowned. The night was dark and a heavy sea running so that he could not be found.

## PORTLAND TRANSCRIPT

### February 5, 1870

On the 21st ult., William Jordan of North Yarmouth, had a fall of twenty feet while taking down an old barn in Cumberland. His skull was fractured and blood vessels ruptured in his head and chest. Dr. Hall was immediately called and did all that medical skill could accomplish, but there was little hope of recovery when correspondent wrote.

John Marshall, a driver on the Rockland and Bath stage line, has driven daily from Portland to Augusta 14 years, and from Bath to Damariscotta 20 years. This amounts to a distance of 430,560 miles, or more that 17 times the circumference of our globe. He is only 58 years old.

There was a serious stabbing affray in Winthrop last week. Robert Taylor, Charles Frost, and Edwin Gouldthrite quarreled while on a drunken spree. Taylor was knocked down with a club and beaten over the head and stabbed just above the hip. The wound is considered dangerous. The assailants picked him up and carried him to his boarding house. The affair happened on the factory bridge.

Capt. Alfred Beals, of the steamer Eastern Queen, was killed in Boston Harbor on Tuesday week, being struck on the head by the walking beam of the steamer. It was his first trip as captain, he being formerly a pilot. He leaves a wife and three children in Hallowell.

Daniel Hodgman of Gilead, recently attempted suicide cutting his throat with a small pocket knife. He did not sever the jugular vein, but his recovery is doubtful.

James Roby, of New Sharon, was killed by a falling tree on the 21st ult.

A. M. Hill of Bridgton met with a quite a serious accident while felling masts in the woods of Col. Perley of South Bridgeton, a limb, falling, striking him upon his fore arm making a wound eight inches in length and extending two thirds round that arm. D. H. Kimball dressed the wound and Mr. Hill will probably lose his arm.

Oliver Evans, of Alfred had his jaws terrible crushed between logs at the saw mill where he was employed, on the 26th ult. Both the upper and lower jaws were broken and lips badly cut.

William Logan, convicted of killing McCarthy at Standish, has been sentenced to six years in the state prison. J. H. Cotton, for rape, goes for life.

Patrick Welch lost his life in a singular way in a logging camp at Telos Lake. He was carrying his axe on his right arm, when the handle of it caught on a passing load of logs in such a way as to cut off his arm above. The men with him were unable to stop the flow of blood and he soon died.

Franklin Maxwell, formerly of Augusta, has arrived at New Sharon where his wife is residing with her father, after a prolonged and romantic residence among the Indians in Colorado. He was taken prisoner and his companions were all killed and scalped. Two of them were Maine men, William Hanson of Readfield, and George Town of Winthrop. He was partly scalped and shows the wounds upon his head. But he had the presence of mind to tell his captors that he had whiskey and tobacco for them, for which his life was spared. This was on the 5th of last March. On the 10th of December he effected his escape. In the meantime, he had adopted their habits and modes of life, in order to keep on good terms with them. We gather these particulars from the Lewiston Journal.

Miss Susan F. Huse of Camden, dropped dead on Wednesday week.

Ruth Coffin has recovered $1800 from the administrator of the late Robert Hull for her services in taking care of him many years; defendants filed a motion to set aside the verdict.

## MARRIAGES

In this city, Jan 25th, Charles H. Babb and Maria E. Loomer, both of the city of Portland.

In this city Jan. 27th, William H. Andrews and Lizzie A. Griffin, both of Portland.

In this city Jan, 25th , James Flynn and Johanna Herbert.

In West Lubec, Jan, 12th, at the residence of the bride's father, by the Rev. Elbridge Pepper, William R. Sleight , Jr. of Sag Harbor, N. Y., Sarah Andrews of West Lubec.

In Lovell, Jan 18th, Preston U. Hamlin, of Sweden and Nellie J. Libby, formerly of Bridgton.

In Hartford Conn., Jan. 29th by Rev. George S. Mallory, J. Fred Cook., formerly of Stevens Plains Me., and Addie N. Malleham, of Wakefield, N. H.

## DEATHS

In this city, of consumption, Mary E. Adams, aged 28.

In this city, Jan 26th, Charles Marriner, aged 41.

In this city, Jan 25th, Mrs. Margaret N. Rolfe, aged 55.

In this city, Jan. 20th, Albert S. Fabyan.

At Sellers Landing, Ill., Dec. 30th after a illness, Mrs. Lydia Howland Smith, aged 70, formerly of Edgecomb, Me.

In East Boston, Jan. 21st, William Hunnewell, only child of William II, and Etta E. Deverson, aged 2 years and 11 months., 7 days.

"O mourn not fond mother for the joys that depart,
There is comfort and peace for the stricken in heart.
God has taken the jewel, that basked in thy love.
The plant that your reared to gladden life's gloom,
Has fastened its root in the soil of the tomb.
It bloomed in your garden, so bright and so fair,
It was climbed o'er the wall and is blooming there.

In Hollis, Dec. 22nd Franklin Woodman, aged 28 years after a short and severe sickness in peace and hope of a glorious immortality.

He was a young man of strict integrity, dearly beloved by his wife, father, mother and only brother and other near acquaintances.

Me thinks I hear him call me now
He bids me meet him there.
In accents soft he speaks and low,
Of joys, where we may share.
Yes loved one, thou'lt again be mine.
Forever mine in Heaven
And thou that star by which I'll find
The road to that blest haven.

## PORTLAND TRANSCRIPT

### February 19, 1870

After Hamblin, the burglar has been boarded in Belfast jail as long as justice demands he is wanted as a boarder in nearly every other jail in the state—he has had such "taking" ways with him in every county, so far as heard from.

The petition of Laura M. Nutt and 71 others of Pembroke for an amendment of the Constitution allowing woman to vote, has been received and referred, which may be considered as the opening of the campaign in this state.

Mr. A. B. McCausland a leading citizen of Farmingdale dropped dead at the house of a relative, last week, aged 40. He was troubled with heart disease.

Henry S. Richards, of Bangor, a file cutter, dropped suddenly dead on his 37th birthday, last Friday.

Mr. James Easton, baggage-master of Kendall's Mills station, on the M.C.R.R. had a serious and singular accident happen to him last week. He was changing the switch, as he supposed in the dark for a regular freight train, but it proved to be a "snow plough train" which took up more room. His foot was caught by a spike at the instep, and he was dragged by several rods through the snow at a speed of twenty or thirty miles an hour. The foot was horribly mangled, and it was necessary to amputate it. The Waterville Mails says he was at last accounts getting on as comfortably as could be expected.

We alluded last week to the attempted escape of two of the Bowdoinham bank robbers. It was Bartlett and not Maguire who accompanied Simms. Simms used a kind of a drill to loosen the bolts of his door and with a key let out Bartlett. From an attic window with a plank they gained the top of the outer wall, and leaped into a short lived freedom. Just then the alarm was given, the snow was deep and their progress was slow. The sentinels after several shots hit Bartlett in the arm and both quietly surrendered. They have kept very close-mouthed ever since. Bartlett's wound was slight.

Frank Richardson, aged 18 was killed at an ice house in Pittson, last week by the fall of a block which was being hoisted.

Mrs. Tryphenia Grindle, of Surry has had three husbands, 12 children, and in all 215 descendants of four generations.

The trial of John Lawrence, for the murder of Mrs. Atwood is in progress at Bangor.

Kennebec had a earthquake all to itself last week, but was no great shakes.

Mr. Smith Chase of Topsham, fell from a platform car, on Sturdivant's wharf on Monday, and fractured two of his ribs.

John Fitz, of Pennsylvania, a veteran of the war of the Revolution and 1812, now 107 years old, visited Congress on Friday and was received with much attention.

Uncle Tommy Houstin, says the Argus, has slaughtered in Portland and vicinity, during his long and prosperous career, over twenty-nine thousand hogs!

Charles Atherton, of Exeter, N. H., was instantly cut in two on Friday, by the bursting of a circular saw with which he was at work.

President Grant's father was seventy-six years old last Sunday. His dutiful son has re-nominated him to be postmaster of Covington, Ky.

## MARRIAGES

In this city Feb. 9th, John A. Appleton, Jr., of Haverhill, Mass., and Ellen M. Robinson, both of Portland.

In this city, Rev. John H. Roberts and Marietta Carey, both of Charlestown, Mass.

In this city, Feb. 5th, Charles A. Freeman and Abbie M. Welch, both of Freeport.

In Cornish, Dec. 4th, by Rev. A Cole, Thaddeus B. Cole, of Limington, and Lydia F. Stone, of Cornish; 5th Moses S. Roberts and Martha E. Weeks, both of Parsonsfield; 7th, Edwin G. Sanborn, of Standish, and Emma E. Norton, of C; 18th Nathan W. Fenderson and Abbie F. Brackett; both of Parsonsfield, 21st. J. Frank Perry, of Cabot,

Vt., and Lizzie P. Swett, of Limerick; Jan, 13th Brackett T. Lord, of C.; and Eliza A. Piper, of Parsonsfield.

In Limington, Feb. 1st, Henry F. Coffin, of Westbrook and Hattie A. Moody, of Limington

In Cape Elizabeth, Rev. 9th, at the residence of the bride's father, by Rev. H. M. Vail, W. Skillin and Rosie F. Marriner, both of Cape. Elizabeth. [The editor returns thanks of a slice of the bridal loaf and wishes the young couple many years of happiness.]

In Searsmont, Feb. 1st., by Rev. H. B. Wardwell, John H. Corey, of Boothbay, and Mary A. Cunningham, of Montville.

In Durham, 22nd, Benjamin L. Small of Pownall and Hettie L. Shaw of Durham.

## DEATHS

In this city, Feb. 13th, Mrs. Eunice Miller, aged 54.
In this city, Feb. 8th, Christina E. Bodkins, aged 10.
In this city, Feb. 10th, Mrs. Mary E. Files, aged 28.
In this city, Feb. 11th, Miss Betsey Thomas, aged 28.
In this city, 10th Enos Parker, of Georgia, Vt., aged 75.
In this city, Feb. 7th, Hannah O' Leary, aged 15.
In this city, Feb, 12th , Capt. Ebenezer Johnson, aged 71.
In this city, Feb. 11th, Mrs. Jane W. Fickett.

In Boston, Feb, 8th, of heart disease, Martin L. son of Thomas Cobb, of Portland, aged 29 years, 2 months, 5 days.

In North Windham, Dec. 18th, Robert Morton, aged 64.

In Windham, Feb. 8th, Mrs. Hannah, wife of Thomas McDonald, aged 53 years, 2 months.

In Chester. N. H., Jan 31st. Henrietta A. Pritham, aged 27.

In Somerville, Mass., Jan 24th , Mrs. Sarah B. Peters, wife of Abraham W. Crowninshield, formerly of Portland.

In Mexico, Feb. 5th , Charles Goff, formerly of Auburn, aged. 21.

## PORTLAND TRANSCRIPT

### February 26, 1870

The storm of Friday night and Saturday was very severe not only in New England, but as far west as Washington, where it alternately rained, hailed and snowed with occasional thunder and lightning. In portions of New Hampshire and Vermont, and especially in this state, the damage done by the flood to bridges, railroad tracks and buildings was very great and the loss is severe. The sudden melting of the snow caused a fearful and inundation which was made more dangerous by the breaking up and clogging of the ice in the river.

The store of John T. Oxnard, of Pownal, was burned on Wednesday week. Total loss. Insured.

The house of stable of Luther Merrill of Caribou, were burnt last week.

Jerome Packard of Camden, who has been living an outlaw's life, using a lonely house in Cushing as a place of resort, has been caught after many unsuccessful attempts on the part of the officers and lodged in Belfast jail. He is accused of four serious and unprovoked assaults.

In the case of Lawrence, tried at Bangor, for the murder of Mrs. Atwood, the jury brought him in guilty after an hour's deliberation. The only defense was insanity. But the evidence showed it to be a case of jealousy, as he was jealous of quite a number of the most respectable citizens of Bangor, among them a deacon. The defense offered to prove that his jealousy was groundless and therefore a proof of insanity. The innocence of the six or eight "respectable men," was allowed by the prosecution, as a matter of fact, but the inference was denied. He prepared himself for the deed by making himself mad with drink, but the pleas of insanity was not helped by this fact, although the defense proved a sunstroke while in the army, and some doctors testified that that might have caused a craving for liquor. The prisoner was not called upon to testify in his behalf.

A man named Walbridge fell dead last Saturday at Bangor, from actual bursting of the heart. A rupture two inches long was found in it.

## MARRIAGES

In this city, Feb. 13th, by Rev. George Tewksbury, Nelson Green and Miss Jane Falkingham, both of Westbrook.

In this city, Feb. 15th, Samuel H. Pike, and Annie I. Van Horn, both of Portland.

In this city, Feb. 14th, by H. C. Houston, Esq., Joshua L. Taylor and Maggie A. Doyle, both of Portland.

In Brownfield, Feb. 20th, by S. B. Bean, Esq. William Smith Haley and Ellen Gray, both of Brownfield.

In East Boston, Feb. 16th, Dr. Richard M. Ingalls and Miss Mary F. Shattuck, both of Boston.

In Auburn, Feb. 7th, E. C. Dunlap, of Westport and Lois M. Hunton of Lewiston.

In Lewiston, Feb. 15th, Emerson E. Goding and Abbie A. Bigelow, both of Livermore Falls.

In Lewiston, Feb. 3rd, Dr. B. F. Sturgis of Auburn and P. Jennie Brooks of Lewiston.

## DEATHS

In this city, Feb. 17th, Hon. William Willis, aged 75.

In this city, Feb.. 20th, Happy Morse, widow of the late Enoch Morse.

In this city. Feb. 16th, Albert Redlon, aged 28 , oldest child of Nathaniel and Jane Redlon.

In this city, Feb. 17th, Frank C. Quincy, aged 20.

In this city Feb. 20th, William B. Small, aged 47.

In this city Feb. 15th, Elijah P. Lewis, aged 36

In this city, Feb. 19th, William Radford, aged. 30

In this city, Feb. 20th, George W. Moody, aged 58.

In this city, Jan. 21st , Lieut. Harrison Holt, 6th , U. S. Cavalry, aged 27.

In this city, Feb. 21, Mrs. Mary Otis, aged 35.

In Cape Elizabeth, Feb. 18th, Mrs. Sarah B. widow of John Willard, aged 80.

In Lebanon, Feb. 5th, James A. Ricker, aged 31 years, 6 months.

Miss Eva Lane of Westbrook Seminary, daughter of one of the overseers in the cotton mills at Saccarappa, died suddenly on Sabbath morning by hemorrhage, the immediate result of exposure on the stormy Saturday on which the Peabody obsequies were had in this city. She was a young lady of culture and high Christian character. *Press.*

PORLTAND TRANSCRIPT

March 5, 1870

The Dover Observer, alluding to the death of J. S. Munroe, Judge of Probate, says that four of the six last judges of that court have died in office.

A fatal stabbing affray occurred at St. George on Wednesday week, originating in a quarrel between a young man named Smalley and another named William Jones. Jones flogged Smalley for insulting him on Tuesday night. The quarrel was renewed the next evening when Smalley was assisted by Edward Andrews, and another person. In the fight which took place Jones was stabbed in several places and died in about twenty minutes. He was able to reach home in time and told his mother that Edwards had stabbed him. Andrews is about twenty years of age and lives at Seal Harbor. He has been arrested and is now in custody of the officers in Thomaston. All the parties to the quarrel were quite young men, and it seems that the quarrel arose at the singing school which they attended.

Eli Aldrich of Greenwood, was drowned together with his team of two horses at Bacon's Falls, West Paris, on the 19th ult. The freshet had thrown a strong current into the road, and he was attempting to drive through it, but the stream was too strong and took him and his team into the river. A boy with him was saved almost by miracle. This is the first loss of life from the late freshets which we had had to record.

General Ames, one of the new Senators from Mississippi, is a Maine man.

Last week Samuel Cram of Windham, attempted suicide by beating his head against a cider press, but was discovered and rescued. The next night when not watched he attempted to cut his throat with a dull knife and was again discovered. He lies in a critical condition. About 10 years ago his brother, Green Cram, committed suicide and only a few weeks ago, a second brother Cabel S. put an end to his own life. A suicidal insanity seem to be hereditary in the family.

John Ward and his wife of Olamon, made a charcoal fire in their room before retiring, on the 23rd ult., and shut the door to keep the dog out. They were found dead in the morning and showed no evidence of any struggles of life. They seemed to be sleeping, no muscle of their faces, showing any evidence of pain. They leave seven children to mourn their loss.

The details of Col. Baker's attack on the Pigeon Indian Village, in Montana, are of a most horrible character. Of 173 killed, only 15 were fighting. They were 90 women and 50 children killed, many of the latter being in the parent's arms. The whole village had been suffering for two months with the small pox, some half dozen dying daily. This butchery of helpless women and children places Baker in the same category of Wirz and Forrest. The massacre is a disgrace to the nation.

## MARRIAGES

In this city, Feb. 23rd, James P. Sherwin and Katie E. Thomas, both of Portland.

In Lewiston, Feb. 20th, Charles C. Brown and Emma C. Rolfe, both of Clinton.

In Lisbon, Feb. 19th, William H. Foster, of Lisbon and Mary T. Jones, of Stafford.

In Biddeford, Feb. 20th Gardiner E. Seavey, of Saco, and Mary A. Sanford of Palmyra.

In Lewiston, Feb. 20th, Thomas W. Brewer of Freeport and Mrs. Narcissa S. Richards of Brewer.

In August, Feb. 16th, Thomas S. Sanford of Bowdoinham and Maggie J. McManus of Brunswick.

In Lewiston, Feb. 20th, Samuel Litchfield and Cynthia Stanford.

## DEATHS

In this city, Feb. 27th, Nellie J. Frohock, aged 19.

In this city, Feb. 25th, Mrs. Clarissa Branscomb, aged 75 years 2 months.

In this city, Feb. 27th, Mrs. Sarah Cobb, aged 75.

In this city, Feb. 27th, Mary E. Duddy, aged 30.

In Westbrook, Jan. 28th, Daniel Woodbury, aged 55.

In Readfield, Feb. 18th, Nancy Taylor, widow of Samuel Greely, aged 75 year, 11 months.

In Windham, Nov. 3rd, Annie C., only daughter of Cyrus and Emily Hawks, aged 14 years, 6 months.

In Lisbon, Feb. 7th, George Hilton, of Wiscasset, aged 67.
In Westbrook, Feb. 24th, John W. Minott, aged 89.
In Westbrook, Feb. 24th, P. Osborne Howe, aged 28.
In Auburn, Feb. 19th, Mrs. Anna, widow of the late John Stockbridge, of Bryon, aged 82.
In Lewiston , Feb. 22nd, Silas S. Cummings, aged 29.
At Cape Elizabeth Ferry, Feb. 9th, Mrs. Almira Skillins, aged 79.
In Cape Elizabeth, Feb. 24, very suddenly, Samuel Burnell, aged 61.
In Denmark, Feb. 25th, Mrs. Miranda E. wife, of J. C. Hodge, and daughter of Ezra Eastman, of Limerick, aged 37.

MEMORANDA

Schooner Abbie, of Yarmouth, Capt. Davis, at New York from Matanzas reports 16th, lat. 30 32, lon 18, had a heavy gale from S S W, stove long boat, filled cabin with water and brig Canima, from Portland for Cuba, which got ashore below Portsmouth, has been found to have sustained no damage and she will proceed the first fair wind.

Schooner Eliza Pike, which was run ashore off Charleston is breaking up. She is valued at $20,000 and the cargo $25,000.

Schooner, Packard, from Wilmington for Baltimore before reported ashore at Ocean View, was got off 21st and towed to Norfolk.

Barque Osmyn, ashore at Whitley's Island, Puget Sound has been abandoned to the underwriters.

Schooner Ratan was driven ashore at Ellsworth Harbor during the gale of the 18th and the schooner Argicols had her main mast carried away.

## PORTLAND TRANSCRIPT

### March 12, 1870

In Washington, on Friday night Hon. John A. Peters, of Maine, discovered a burglar in his bedroom rifling his pockets, but the fellow escaped. He had stolen $560 from Senator Morrill of Vermont and two gold watches and $75 from Senator Ferry who board in the same house.

Several weeks ago two convicts at the Thomaston prison got into a quarrel in which Hickey got Murphy's thumb into his mouth and chewed it badly. Murphy was so ashamed of the manner of getting his wound that he made no complaint about it but kept at work washing. The result was that inflammation set in, and last week his right arm was amputated above the elbow. The Rockland Gazette says his recovery is still doubtful.

Roscoe G. Newell, whose mysterious disappearance in Oct. 1865 caused great anxiety among his friends, died a few days ago in New Jersey, revealing his name just before his death. He was a son of Sumner R. Newell of Paris.

Patrick Berry was killed and two fellow laborers seriously injured by the fall of an embankment on the P. &. R. railroad in Sanford, last week.

Nathaniel Harlow of Bangor, aged about 90, followed his fifth wife to the grave last Saturday.

J. D. Kent, of Brewer, was found dying in his berth on board of the Katahdin, on Saturday week, when the waiters went to make up the berth. He died just after the boat left Belfast.

The house and barn of Silas Dickerson, of Edgecomb, was burned on the 24th ult.

The first cotton mill in Maine was started at Brunswick in 1811 by Joshua Herrick, who is now living at Alfred and who writes to the Argus an account of the enterprise. Mr. Herrick was deputy sheriff in this county during the last year of our connection with Massachusetts.

The sudden and afflictive death of Miss Nellie J. Forhock on Monday week, has cast a deep shade over the family of which she was a most worthy ornament and the large circle of friends who were bound to her by the golden chain of friendship. Her powers of composition were unusual, for she could not only express her ideas freely but with great beauty of form. Her parents gave her an excellent education, and she was one of the class of '69 in the Portland High School who seemed to be the greatest promise. Talented, studious, modest, pure-minded, she must have endeared herself to her friends with a tender regard, and when added to all these attractive qualities her religious nature was early and sincerely developed, it could hardly be otherwise than that her classes should have had a high respect and true love for her. Her funeral was very largely attended, and as she lay so beautiful in death, the great poet's description of Greece, and as compared to the corpse of a beautiful person, was most forcibly impresses upon the mind:

"Here is the loveliness in death
That parts not quite with parting breath;
But beauty with that fearful bloom,
The hue which haunts it to the tomb,
Expression's last receding ray,
A gilded halo hovering round decay
The farewell beam of Feeling passes away,
Spark of that flame perchance of heavenly birth
Which gleams, but warms no more its cherished earth."

### MARRIAGES

In this city, Mar. 5th, Hiram T. Plummer and Mrs. Louis S. Drew, both of Portland.

In this city, March 7th, H. Frank Robinson, of Frederickton, N. B. and Nellie A. Merrill, of Portland

In Westbrook, March 1st by Rev. J. C. Snow, Charles Matthews of Westbrook, and Miss Jane N. Simpton, of Portland.

In Westbrook, March 3rd, Hon. Stephen D. Lindsey and Mary M. Clarke, both of Norridgewock.

In Biddeford, March 3rd., Oswell Charles and Eliza M. Manchester, both of Biddeford.

In Kennebunk, James L. Cummings and Margarette Nettle, both of Portland.

In Saco, Feb. 8th, Rev. John Boothby of Saco and Mary Manson, of Limington.
In Stockton, Wilson S. Kneeland and Ellen M. Macomber.
In Norway, Feb. 5th, George W. Bonney and Mrs. E. L. Davis.
In Runford Center, Feb. 8th, James W. Thomas, Jr., and Frances E. Pillsblow.

## DEATHS

In this city, March 2nd, Mary O'Connell, aged 20.
In this city, March 2nd, Charles Deehan, aged 58.
In this city, March 4th, Josiah B. Snow, aged 39.
In this city, March 6th, Augusta F. Deane, aged 18.
In North Yarmouth, Feb, 27, Rufus Porter, aged 59 years, 10 months.
In Westbrook, March 3rd, Lester Alexander Bailey, aged 13.
In York, Feb. 27th, Mrs. Edner D. Coche, aged 60 years, 10 months. [Boston papers please copy.]
In Tripoli, Barbary, Dec. 28th, William Porter, Esq., American Consul-formerly of Portland.
In Freeport, Nathaniel Nye, aged 90.
In Topsham, Mrs. Sarah Sumner, aged 35.
In Rockland, Feb. 7th, Mrs . Sarah Simmons, aged 80.
In Biddeford, Mrs. Maria S. Garland, aged 29.
In Cape Elizabeth, March 2nd Henry L. Nelson, aged 27,
In Vassalboro, Feb. 16th James H. Blanchard, aged 90.
In Gorham, Feb. 26th, Mrs. Elizabeth G. Kellogg, aged 64.
In Searsport, Feb. 13th Putnam Simonton, M. D., aged 57.

In Oquawka, Ill., Feb. 26th, Elisha Hinds formerly of Portland, aged 70 years and 6 months. [Boston papers please copy.]

> Underneath the sod low lying
> Dark and drear
> Sleepth one who left in dying
> Sorrow here.
>
> Rest in peace thou gentle Spirit
> Throned above
> Souls like thine with God inherit
> Life and love.

# PORTLAND TRANSCRIPT

## March 10, 1870

Mr. Nathaniel Stevens a respected citizen residing on Portland Street, died suddenly in his bed on Thursday morning of last week; he was apparently in his usual good health the day before; he was 65 years old, and was well known in connection with the wool business.

On Thursday week, Capt. Edward Robinson, residing on Chestnut Street, sent his housekeeper out on an errand, and when she went back she found him hanging by the neck dead; he was a retired shipmaster, who had amassed a handsome competency, but had met with losses and been unfortunate in business, which probably preyed upon his mind and led to the commission of the rash deed. He was 52 years old and unmarried.

A young man named John Brooks from New Hampshire was killed at Danville last week while shackling cars.

Two young men from Brunswick named J. W. Alexander and William Cooper went to Bath on Saturday week, became drunk and had a fight. Next morning Alexander was found at Cook's Crossing with his throat gashed in eight places and his feet so badly frozen that they may have to be amputated. Cooper was arrested on charges of assault with intent.

A terrible accident occurred at Biddeford last Saturday afternoon. Oliver Tracy agent of the West Buxton, woolen mills, John J. Sawyer, a lumber dealer of Hollis and H. Partridge, of Saco, attempted to cross the railroad in a sleigh drawn by a pair of horses, when the locomotive of the Boston train was not over fifty feet away. Mr. Partridge was driving and they were all so muffled up that the did not hear the whistle. The horses cleared the track but the cow-catcher struck the sleigh, throwing all the occupants high in the air. Mr. Tracey was found near the fence badly mangled, and dead–his death must have been instantaneous. Mr. Sawyer was on the cow-catcher, insensible, with a fractured skull; Mr. Partridge was on top of him, uninjured but greatly bewildered–his first exclamation being that he lost his hat. Mr. Sawyer was conveyed to the residence of his sister in Saco, and died in a few hours. No blame is attached to the engineer who did his best to warn them and to stop his locomotion.

## MARRIAGES

In this city, Mar. 14th, William H. Gould and Alice Wood, both of Portland.

In this city, Mar. 9th, by Rev. W. H. Fenn, Deloss Davison, of New York and Maria L. Hall, of Portland.

In this city, March 8th, James G. Meserve and Esther F. Meserve, both of Gorham.

In this city, James E. Smith and Celia A. Ellis, both of Portland.

In Alfred, Mar. 10th by Rev. George Lewis and Mr. H. Paris Smith and Clarrie M. Grant, both of Lyman.

In Gorham, Mar. 10th, by Rev. S. B. Sawyer, William Wiley Davis and Emily Frances Wescott, both of Gorham.

In Turner, Feb. 18th Amory H. Allen and Nellie A. Merrill.

In Biddeford. Feb.20th Frank L. Taxbor and Lizzie Tyler.

In Farmington, Mar. 5th, John C. Whitmore and Charlotte A. Graves.

In Pittsfield, Mar. 5th, L. F. Foss and L. A. Tripp.

## DEATHS

In this city, Mar. 11th, Mary Scribner, only daughter of John Lough, aged 30.

In this city, Mar. 12th, Enoch Jones, aged 46.

In this city, Mar. 10th very suddenly Nathaniel Stevens, aged 66.

In this city, Mar. 10th Capt. Edward Robinson, aged 52.

In this city, Mar. 20th Nathaniel Welden, aged 77.

In this city, Mar. 7th Marion, infant daughter of Henry M. and Emma C. Payson.

In Westbrook, Mar. 14th, Nathan Hilton, Jr. formerly of Bridgton, aged 47 years and 10 months.

In Dallas, Oregon, Mar. 3rd, Mrs. Fannie G., wife of James B. Crosson, and daughter of the late Capt. Jacob Gray of North Yarmouth, Me.

In San Rafael, Cal. 11th, Capt. Daniel L. Choate, of Portland.

PORTLAND TRANSCRIPT

March 26, 1870

Charles Westcott fell overboard from Custom Wharf on Monday and was rescued from drowning by Officer Houston and others.

We regret to learn that Miss Ella Goddard, a daughter of Col. John Goddard of Cape Elizabeth, died of scarlet fever at Westbrook Seminary on Sunday last, after an illness of a little more than a week; her sister, Miss Minnie Goddard, who went to the Seminary boarding house to attend her sister, has also been taken down with the same disease.

The American ship Ventres from Callao, with guano, for Antwerp, has been lost on the coast of Belgium, she belonged in Thomaston, Me.

Gen. Hersey of Bangor, seems to be the "coming man", of the republican government.

Master Walter Sargent of the Oneida, was a native and former resident of Gouldsboro. He was married at Brooklyn, N. Y., one week before he sailed for Japan.

A Gardiner lad, named Whitmore, shot himself through the hand while playing with a pistol on Friday night.

G. W. K. Brown, of South Lincoln, lost his house and three barns by fire last week.

Officer C. M. Wormell, of Bethel, has been doing a good business in reclaiming stolen horses of late. That seems to be his *forte*.

Theodore Nicklas, a youth of eighteen years, was hanged for murder at Little Valley, N. Y., on Friday week.

Mr. Madison Wright, of Mt. Vernon, lost his barn, horse and three cows, by fire on the 14th inst. At Etna, the buildings of Henry McLaughlin was destroyed on the 15th.

Mr. Cake is a member of Congress from Pennsylvania. He must be the last of the dough faces.

The Catholic priests of Madrid refused to officiate at the funeral of Prince Henri de Bourbon because there were Masonic emblems on his coffin.

The trial of Pierre Bonaparte for the homicide of Victor Noir has commenced at Tours.

## MARRIAGES

In this city, Mar. 16th, Levi T. Cummings and Lizzie R. Waite, both of Portland.

In this city, Mar. 16th, Eben L. Huston, of Falmouth and Julia C. L. Foot, of Portland.

In this city, Mar. 16th, Isaac Small, of Cornish and Vesta S. Doe, of Milford.

In this city, Mar. 16th, James H. Hanselpacker and Clara C. Hinkley.

In Westbrook, Mar. 16th by Rev. J. C. Snow, Fred A. Pollock and Jennie M. Legrow, both of Westbrook.

In Gorham, Feb. 23 rd, George M. Way , of Portland and Lucy P. Patrick, of Gorham.

In Windham, Mar. 6th, Benjamin Small and Isabel Small both of Windham.

In North Yarmouth, March 13th, J. P. Westcott of Gorham, and Clara J. Sawyer, of Pownal.

In Gray, Mary 13th, Gilbert Small of Windham, and Sophia Frank of Gray.

In Biddeford, March 14th George A. Johnson and Mary Gray.

In Brunswick, Mar, 3rd, Edwin B. Clark and Terris A. Toothaker,

In Richmond, Stephen W. Reed, and Marcia R. Alexander.

## DEATHS

In this city, Mar. 16th, Mrs. Phebe Campbell, aged 92.

In this city, Mar. 11th, Mrs. Mary Scribener, aged 30.

In Westbrook, Mar. 20, at the Seminary Ella H., youngest daughter of Col. John and Lydia Goddard, aged 17.

In Yarmouth, on Mar. 9th Mrs. Mariam D., wife of Capt. Jeremiah Buxton, aged 64 years and 8 months.

In Winthrop, Mar. 9th, Samuel C. Blanchard, aged 32.
In Biddeford, Mar. 4th, Abigail S. Rumery, aged 72.
In Saco, Mar. 5th, Joseph Jacobs, aged 64.
In Skowhegan, Mar. 16th Mrs. Emma Libby, aged 28.
In Westbrook, Mar 14th, Nathan Hilton, Jr. aged 48.
In Green, Mar. 18th, Mrs. Mercy Sprague, aged 80.

In this city, May 20th, Charlie E. youngest son of Charles W. and Ellen Roach, aged 8 years 8 months.

>Mother, dear, not dead–I love thee
>Better far than when on earth
>And with tender care above thee,
>Watch I, since my angel birth.

In Cape Elizabeth, Mar. 15th Harry, youngest child of Joseph T. and Ellen M. Darling, aged 3 years 5 months.

>I 've lost my love, my cherished little one
>Who smiling pratting, clasped his mother's knee.
>Alas! His transient hour of life is run,
>And his sweet face and smile are nought to me.

In Lisbon, March 12th, Charles Rogers, aged 79 years 9 months.

>Dear father has left us and passed on before
>And is waiting to greet us on the bright shining shore
>The casket that bore him will crumble away,
>The jewel immortal can never decay.

Portland Transcript

ABBOTT, A. R. 60 Clare E.
109 F. E. 4 H. B. 45 49
Helen M. 65
ADAMS, B. N. 83 Ellen
O.. 91 Esther V. 37 J. C
99 109 J. W. 62 Mary
E. 119 Mrs. 99
ALBEE, Samuel 66
ALBY, Randall 103
ALDRICH, Eli 125
ALEXANDER, J. W. 131
Marcia R. 134
ALLAN, J. D. 53
ALLANES, William W. 62
ALLEN, Amory H. 132
Eliza C. 80 T. Coleman
105 William 21 22
ALLEY, Rose 106
AMBROSE, R. S. 101
AMES, A. L. 57 Dana
L. 57 David 23 Etta
M. 112 General 125
Mary E. 57 Mr. 48
Noah 102
ANDERSON, Horace 95
Mary A. 10 William 1
ANDREWS, 21 Abner L.
73 Edward 125 Hannah
E. 32 Leonard 19 Rev. Mr.
112 Samuel A. 79 Sarah
119 William H. 118
ANNIS, Mary A. 10
APPLETON, John A., Jr. 121
ARMSTRONG, John B. 83
ARNO, Mrs. 64 William 64
ARNOLD, Joseph 100
ASTOR, John Jacob 8
ATHERTON, Charles 121
ATKINSON, Chris G. 57
Rev. Mr. 115
ATWOOD, Mrs. 121 123
AUSTIN, 72 Albert S. 28
Almena S. 28 Charles 2
Ella J. 28 Georgiana 96

AUSTIN (continued)
Leslie 68
AVERY, James 105
AYER, G. W. P. 1 J. B. 1
BABB, Charles 16 Charles
H. 118 David W. 17 Erther
A. 17 Isaac 52 J. W. 41
Maria A. 41
BACKUS, A. 100
BACON, Jabez 76
BAILY, Annie M. 45 B. H. 45
Carrie B. 100 Elbridge G.
112 Francis H. 99 Helen
105 Henriette W. 83 Isabel
W. 79 John 83 Lester
Alexander 130 Ruth 66
S. E. 79
BAKER, Charles B. 45 Col.
126 George H. 97 Henry
111 Mrs. 77 Sally 50
BALL & Smith 14
BALDWIN, Merritt 83
BANGOR House 67
BARBOUR, Officer 109
BARD, Rebecca A. 78
BARDISH, John L. 109
BARKER, Caleb 26 Daniel
W. 27 Fannie M. 65 J.
Perly J. 37
BARNES, Eliza Ellen 50
BARRETT, George 81
BARROWS, Frank R. 96
BARTER, Alden B. 56
BARTLETT, 120 Abbie C. 73
Joseph 31 Rev. Mr. 10
BARTON, Clara 99 Joe 98
BASSETT, Joseph 66
BATCHELDER, David 63
BATES, Hattie D. 115 James
M. 33
BAVIS, Lydia 61
BAYLEY, Frank T. 83
BEAL, Isaac N. 10
BEALE, Rufus 110 Samuel

Portland Transcript

BEALE (continued)
N. 74
BEALS, Alfred 117 Eveline
73
BEAN, E. 61 78 Franklin
51 Richard H. 61 S. B.
124 Shepard 72 Watson
D. 102
BEARCE, Henry M. 2
BEAUREGARD, Gen. 36
BECKETT, Sarah A. 54
BEECHER, Henry Ward 26
BELCHER, Rachel 55
BELL, Nellie J. 41
BELLOWS, Mary L. 41
BENEUIT, Lewey 76
BENNER, A. V. 28 Addie
V. 28 O. 28
BENNETT, Mr. 68 Thomas
59
BENSON, Fannie 29 Rev.
Mr. 109
BENT, Samuel A. 65
BERRIGAN, 108
BERRY, Andrew G. 90
Carrie 45 Flavilla 78
George S. 29 James 45
john 43 Maria 109 Maria
F. 29 Patrick 128
Villa A. 78
BEVERIDGE, Elmer 25
BIBBER, William B. 115
BICKFORD, F. W. 55
BIGELOW, Abbie A. 124
Betsey G. 73
BIGFORD, Isaac 114
BILLINGS, Ivory H. 66
Mercy 1 Samuel 17
Thomas 17
BINFORD, Deblois N. 27
BISBEE, Jonas 102
BLACK, M. E. 106
BLADGON, Benjamin 66
BLAINE, J. B. 6 J. G. 67

BLAISDELL, Daniel D. 102
Nathaniel 48 Vesta A. 47
51
BLAKE, 26 Annie M. 100
Benjamin 33 Caleb 65
Charles B. 65 Ella S. 113
Ephriam S. 24 Gorham G.
7 Harvey 80 Nancy 74
BLANCHARD, James H. 130
Lydia 99 Samuel C. 135
Sarah J. 61
BLETHEN, George B. 60
BLISS, Gershom 115
BLODGETT, SEPPIE k. 112
BLOOD, Horatio 65
BODGE, Abbie M. 106
BODKINS, Christina E. 222
BOLES, E. C. 41 (3) 16
BONAPARTE, Pierre 134
BOND, George 57
BONHALL, Capt. 80
BONNER, Thomas 69
BONNEY, George W. 130
BOOTH, Edwin 44 John 41
John Wilkes 53
BOOTHBY, Alexander 73
Ellen S. 28 John 130
BORCHERS, E. F. 106
BOTTS, John Minor 20
BOUTWELL, Charles H. 65
BOWDEN, P. 62
BOWEN, 62 Hiram A.
16 John 53 P. 62 Oliver,
Jr. 46
BOWMAN, Emily A. 65
BOYD, A. P. 42 Fred L. 10
BOYNTON, Gardner B. 91
Sarah Belle 91 Sarah J. 91
BRACKETT, 48 Abbie F. 121
Edward 80 John 33 Lionel
115
BRADBURY, Alice 106
Benjamin 96 H. J. 33 37
49 83 106 112

Portland Transcript

BRADEEN, 59 Filena A. 58
BRADLEY, David 55 Edith
  61 F. G. 83 John 61
  Josephine 61 Samuel A. 61
BRANCROFT, Addie 91
BRANNING, Thomas 77
BRANSCOMB, Clarissa 126
BRAY, Jacob 87
BREED, Lewis C. 103
BREWER, Thomas W. 126
BRIGGS, Annett W. 65
  Horace A. 57 Joseph 109
BRIMIGEON, Phebe 113
BROOKS, Alfred 35 Charles
  M. 10 John 131 P. Jennie
  124
BROPHY, James 82
BROWN, Caroline 14
  Charles C. 126 F. W. 43
  G. W. K. 133 Isaac H. 99
  J. I. 37 Lizzie S. 73 Nellie
  T. 37 Oliver 88 Rebecca 45
  William 95
BRUCE, Frederick 41
BRYANT, 63 Ann 56
  Sarah E. 41
BUCK, Charlotte 42
  George H. 51 J. L.
  66
BUCKNAM, Amos 10
  Lydia 10 William H. 10
BUEHRER, Arthur 56
BULLOCK, John T. 41
BUNKER, 62 B. & Co. 13
BURBANK, Sophia 57
BURGESS, Bishop 90
BURKE, John H. 91
BURKAR, Martha J. 27
BURLEIGH, Albert P. 65
  J. E. 79
BURNELL, Samuel 127
BURRILL, Jonas D. 28
BUSHER, Lovell 23
BUSHEY, Isaac 91

BUTLER, 37 Allie 103
  John 79 Mary A. 96
BUTTERFIELD, Jonas 91
BUXTON, Dr. 86 Jeremiah
  134 Mariam D. 134
BUZZELL, William W. 57
BYTHER, D. B. 37
CADE, Elizabeth 71
CAHOON, George W. 73
CAKE, Mr. 134
CALDWELL, J. W. 44
CALL, Joseph F. 50
CALLAHAN, George A. 88
  Lotta B. 88 Nettie B. 88
CALLAO, 58
CAMERON, Lydia P. 88
CAMPBELL, Harvey 95
  Jennie M. 83 John 112
  Phebe 134
CAPEN, Henry T. 53
CAPEON, 6
CAREY, Marietta 121
CARLETON, Charles A. 112
CARLLTON, Sarah 83
  Wesley W. 73
CARNEY, Alice W. 16 Hattie
  A. 16 W. C. G. 16
CARR, Gilman 94 James O.
  112
CARROLL, Ella 45 Georgie
  10
CARRUTHERS, Edwin J. 87
CARSLEY, William 106
CARTER, C. P. & Co. 74
  Daniel 58 Henry 63
CARY, Annie 90 Georgie A.
  69 James 14
CAUSER, William 106
CEZEER, Clara 65
CHAFFEE, Sophia L. 46
CHAMBERLAIN, Caroline
  A. 41 George 110 Governor
  1 33 40 63 86 Samuel 66
CHANDLER, D. H. 69 Sarah

Portland Transcript

CHANDLER (continued)
Emma 69 Zebedee 72
CHANZEY, Perez 102
CHAPLIN, M. D. 101
CHAPMAN, C. E. 37
Emmons 114 Fannie E. 37
T. H. 37
CHAPPEL, Horace 95
CHARLES, Oswell 129
Simeon 51
CHASE, Adaline A. 84
Alfred 61 Geneva 66
Irena C. 61 Lucretia 45
Lucy A. 61 Smith 121
Stephen Henry 44
Superintendent 24
W. T. 78 William H.
84
CHENERY, Emma E. W.
95
CHENEY, Mr. 68
CHICK, Ernestine 109
Isaiah 2 Nellie P. 99
Thomas 39
CHOATE, Daniel L. 132
CILLEY, Abigail 103
Benjamin 103 D. C. 103
CLARK, Aaron 3 Ai 39
Cornelia F. 16
Daniel 81 Edwin 111
Edwin B. 134 George B.
88 Mary E. 28 Mr. 2
Thomas 65 Mary M.
129
CLAY, Joseph 83 Lizzie
M. 83 Mary E. 83
CLEAVES, Huldah 113
Thomas 16
CLIFFORD, William 89
CLOUDMAN, Nathan 51
CLOUGH, Isaac 86
CLUFF, Ruth 79
William H. 99
COBB, Edward 91

COBB (continued)
Frankie W. 84 G. F.
84 L. A. 84 Martin L.
122 Sarah 126 Thomas
122 Wright & Norton 15
COBURN, George M. 112
COCHE, Edner D. 130
COE, Charles 24
COFFIN, Almira L. 84
Carrie A. 109 Henry F.
122 Melvina D. 84
Ruth 118 William H. 84
COGGINS, George W. 50
COLBURN, Mary F. J. 106
COLBY, Franklin H. 49
COLE, 31 A. 27 121 D. H. 73
99 Edward 90 George 90
S. L. 40 Thaddeus B. 121
Wallace D. 73
COLESWORTHY, Samuel
H., Jr. 115
COLLEY, Joseph F. 78
COLLINS, James 8 John 62
COLLY, James 20
COLOMY, Abram 50
COLSON, Capt. 74
CONANT, Soloman 74
CONNER, Selden 83
COOK, D. L. 36 J. Fred 119
J. H. 63 John 30 Thomas 2
Victoria E. 50 William H.
80
COOLBROTH, Mary S. 99
COOLEY, D. H. 27 Julia F.
19 William 59
COOLIDGE, Cleora F. 114
Joseph 27
COOMBS, Rachel 51
COOPER, William 131
COREY, John H. 122
CORSER, Margaret Ellen
105 S. T. 105
COTTON, J. H. 118
COUNCE, Margaret F. 87

COUNTY, William 14
COUSINS, Alfred S. 50
COVELL, Frank E. 54
COX, George F. 43 Rev.
  Dr. 16 Samuel A. 66
CRAIG, Amanda 44 45
  Miss 45
CRAM, Cabel S. 125
  Charles 24 Green 125
  Levi 19 Mary J. 50
  Samuel 125
CRANE, David 105
CRAWFORD, James B. 6
  Mr. 41
CREG, Gasgel A. 69
CRESSY, Caroline 84
  Elizabeth A. 74
CROCKETT, Georgie A. C. 56
CROOKER, George 56
  Maria L. 27
CROSBY, John 89
CROSSMAN, Charles C. 83
CROSSON, Fannie G. 132
  James B. 132
CROWELL, Harvey S. 90
CROWINSHIELD, Abraham W. 122
CROWLEY, John 19
CULLINEN, H. & P. 75
CUMMINGS, Amelia C. 79
  George 12 George M. 78
  Hannah S. 10 James L. 129
  Leonard F. 10 Levi T. 134
  Mr. 63 Silas 127 Susie 10
CUNNINGHAM, Mary A. 122 Mrs. 82 N. T. 116
CURRIER, A. H. 91 Isaac M. 79
CURTIS, Charles 73 George 40 56 Irene 79 Jeremiah 13 John 103 Louise A. 46
  Marcilla 49 Susan W. 56
CUSHING, 21 J. Henderson

CUSHING (continued)
  78 Sarah 10
CUSHMAN, Adna T. 87
  Flora A. 96 Gideon 88
CUSKLEY, Alice 69 Martin 69 Sarah I. 69
CUTTER, Fannie L. 80
  Simeon 33
CUTTS, Charles 14
  Mrs. 69
DAGGET, William 58
DALE, Joseph 28
DALTON, A. 87 90 99 105 114 Sarah A. 42
DALY, Peter 100
DAMON, Ruth 73
DAMRELL, Adaline 82
DANA, George W. 50
DARBY, Capt. 39
DARLING, Ellen M. 135
  Harry 135 Joseph T. 135
DAVENPORT, 31
DAVID, Julia H. 73
DAVIDSON, Deloss 132
  Henry 37
DAVIS, Ann 106 Annie E. 50
  Benjamin 104 Betsey 58
  Capt. 127 Charles S. 88
  David A. 75 E. L. 130
  Frank 19 Jeff 32 53 Joe 32
  Julia O. 45 Nathan S. 57
  Rosa C. 103 Reuben 31
  Sylvia 61 Una L. 33
  William Wiley 132
DAWES, T. J. 12
DAY, Edith R. 29
DE BOURBON, Henri 134
DEAN, Henry C. 19
DEANE, Augusta F. 130
DEARBORN, Mr. 81
DECOSTER, Cyrena 56
DEEHAN, Charles 130
DEERING, Alphonso 86
  Emily E. 9 16 John 79 103

Portland Transcript

DEERING (continued)
Mary E. 87 91 Rufus 9 16
DELANO, 36 62
DEMERIT, A. M. 100
DENISON, A. C. & Co. 101
A. T. 101
DENNISON, Charles W. 17
Freddie W. 17
DESISLE, Isaac B. 54
DEVERSON, Etta E. 119
William Hunnewell 119
William II 119
DEWEY, Ellen H. 74
DICKERSON, Silas 128
Sarah 91
DICKSON, Richard Osborne 79
DINGLEY, Fuller 90
DINSMORE, A. M. 102
DIXON, Charles J. 83
DOCKHAM, George N. 106
DODGE, Albert 24 25
Ezekiel G. 62
DOE, Vesta S. 134
DOLAN, James 58 John 109
DOLE, Olive M. 65
DONNEL, Bailey 52
DONNELL, Moses J. 56
DONNELLY, Nettie 73
DOUGLASS, Walter 112
DOW, Maria 106 Neal 99
DOWNEY, 39
DOYLE, Adelaide S. 83
Jane Elizabeth 106
Maggie A. 124 Peter 12
DRESSSER, Clayton D. 61
Mary S. 82
DREW, Louis S. 129
DRUMMOND, David H. 45
Mary E. 57
DUDDY, Mary E. 126
DUNHAM, R. 34 72
DUNLAP, E. C. 124

DUNN, 40 58 C. K. 66
Charles F. 35 D. M. C. 66 Frank Howard 66
DUNTON, John 43 Joseph H. 96 Josiah 55 Laura A. 87
DURAN, F. A. 57
DURGIN, Abigail 46
Samuel 91 W. C. 72
DWIGHT, Annie 102
DYER, Lucy A. 82
EASTMAN, Brothers 36
EASTMAN, B. M. 36 Mr. 93 Ezra 127
EASTON, D. A. 105
H. F. 69 James 120
EATON, Cyrus H. 45 Mr. 77
EBEN, Lizzie 28
EDES, Robert 112
EDSON, Newell W. 45
EDWARDS, J. M 106
Roger 99
ELLIOT, Betsey R. 46
Charles 99 Hannah 97
ELLIS, Celia A. 132 Ella R. 56 Hiram 56
ELMS, Sarah 55
EMERSON, Henry 87
Ralph Waldo 15
EMERY Hotel, 72
EMERY, A. F. 109 Anna E. 74 Edgar 105 Emily 106 Howard 66 Rhoda P. 27 William 93
ERSKINE, 71
EUSTIS, Lewis B. 46 Mary A. 46 Willie H. 46
EVANS, Eunice 28 Oliver 118
EVELETH, John 36
FABYN, Alert S. 119
FAIRBANKS, Alexander H. 41
FALKINGHAM, Jane 124

FALLON, James E. 45
FARLEY, C. H. 99
FARNHAM, Benjamin 51
FARRAR, 101
FARRINGTON, Emeline 103
FAULKNER, Eliza L. 50
FAVOR, Claudia 7
FELLOWS, Rev. Mr. 61
FENDERSON, Collins B. 49
   Nathan W. 121
FENN, W. H. 73 82 91 (2) 95
   105
FERNALD, Ann Eloise 91
   Annie S. 103 N. S. 91
   Susan J. 91
FESSENDEN, Caroline 61
   Senator 72
FIELD, E. D. 83 Ophelia
   E. 83
FIELDS, James A. 79
FILES, Mary E. 122
FINN, Mrs. 31
FINLEY, Nina Van
   Renselaer 45
FINNEGAN, 96
FISH, Charles 31
FISHER, Mrs. 26
FITCH, Emma B. 115
FITZ, John 121
FLANDERS, Rev. Dr. 37
FLETCHER, Abol 39
   Ell M. 65 John 114
FLINT, Charles 40 Sally 87
   William 87
FLOYD, Nancy Jane 16
FLYNN, James 118
FOGG, Charles E. 116
   George 95 Miranda 61
FOLGER, Edmund C. 61
FOLLETT, Lucy F. 50
FOLSOM, M. N. 94
   Rufus H. 51
FOOT, Julia C. L. 134
FOOTE, Lendall G. L. 84

FORBES, Emma J. 28
FORHOCK, Nellie J. 129
FORREST, 126
FOSS, Fannie M. 73
   G. L. 5 Henry 64 L. F.
   132 Martin 57 Susan 115
FOSTER, Albert S. 46 Frank
   108 Lester 108 William H.
   126
FOWLEY, B. F. 6
FOWLER, George 3
   Jeremiah 32
FRANCIS, Nathaniel L. 57
FRANK, Sophia 134
FREDERIC, Henry 87
FREEMAN, A. W. 79
   Charles A. 121 Mary C.
   87 Moses 23 Nathan 87
   Watson 49
FREEZE, Dr. 108
FRENCH, Betsey 42 Clara
   H. 74 Edna 12 George 74
   Julia 57 Margaret S. 74
   Moses 12
FROHOCK, Nellie J. 126
FROST, Carrie W. 79
   Charles 117 Emeline 28
   Hiram 37 John 28 Mary S.
   96 O. C. 64
FRYE, William 7
FULLER, Ben 88 David B.
   28 34 Henry M. 28 34
   Margaret J. 42 Mary 28
   Mary Jane 34 Thomas
   F. 99
FURBISH, Mary F. 106
FURBUR, Benjamin 20
GAGE, Amos 29 Mrs. 5
   Richard 5
GALLISON, Henry, Jr. 110
GAMMON, George Q. 73
GAMMONS, Joseph
GARDINER, Thomas 55
GARDNER, Stephen 61

GAREY, Charles B. 46
GARLAND, David 37
  Maria S. 130
GARLIC, Elizabeth 41
GATES, C. H. 103
GATLEY, Mary J. 33
GAY, Elijah 96 Seth 108
GEARY, Gov. 33
GERALD, Lorenzo 76
GERRARD, Henry 99
GERTS, Martin 46
GIBBON, Michael 40
GIBSON, Arthur 13 Milton 13
GIGGER, Agnes 33
GILBRETH, Benjamin 98
GILE, Augusta C. 57
GILES, Mary J. 56 Stephen 44
GILKEY, 15
GILMORE, Charles 66
GILPATRICK, Mary Ellen 104
GODDARD, Ella 133 Ella H. 134 John 133 134 Judge 77 78 111 Lydia 134 Minnie 133 Robert 68
GODFREY, John F. 73 Martha W. 83
GODING, Emerson E. 124 Harrison 51
GOFF, Charles 122
GOING, Charles 47
GOOD, Margaret 106
GOODWIN, Charles 68
GOOLD, Mary 57
GOULD, Edward F. 51 Martha M. 79 Miss 60 William H. 132
GOULDTHRITE, Edwin 117
GOWEN, Charles C. H. 83 David H. 83 Lucy A. 83
GRACE, Eddie F. 116

GRACE (continued)
  J. P. 116 Martha B. 116
GRAFFAM, Daniel P. 91
  Edwin W. 79 Robert 111
GRANT, Clarrie M. 132
  General 7 20 I. M. 34
  Mrs. 15 President 44 121
  William 60 61
GRAVES, Charlotte A. 132
  Elizabeth C. 49
GRAW, Edward 40
GRAY, 32 Charles E. 74
  Ellen 124 Hattie A. 115
  Jacob 132 Mary 134
GREATON, Widow 39
GREELEY, Horace 7
GREELY, Samuel 126
GREEN, Ellen S. 95 John S. 106 Nelson 124
GREENE, Catharine S. 34 C. H. 41
GREENLEAF, William 6
GREENWOOD, Rodolph 91
GRIFFIN, Edward P. 112
  John 89 Lizzie A. 118
  Martha A. 29
GRINDLE, Tryphenia 121
GROSS, Grenville M. 49
GUPTIL, Ellen A. 82 Sarah 47
HADLEY, Edwin 16
HAINES, G. A. 93
HALE, Ella F. 54 John 40
  John P. 16 Joseph 10
HALEY, Anna M. 50
  Cornelius 72 John J. 61
  William Smith 124
HALL, Adelaide E. 61
  Alfred 108 Annie G. 50
  C. 66 Charles F. 61
  Dr. (2) 75 117 Ellen E. 69 F. S. 50 Lizzie 23 Maria L. 132 Olive 50 Solomon 18 W. 60 W. H. 66 Zemro 23

143

Portland Transcript

HALLERON, Daniel 45
HALLISEY, Joanna 2
HAM, Herrick 18 Mary R. 47
HAMBLIN, 120 Leander D. 54
HAMILTON, Capt. 12
  Georgiana 45 Sylvanus 27
  William 109
HAMLIN, Hannibal 99
  Preston U. 119 Senator 67
HAMMONS, George 97
HANES, Susie F. 50
HANLEY, Robert 49
HANNA, George F. 83
HANNAFORD, Augustus F. 27
HANSCOM, J. & Son 63
HANSELPACKER, James H. 134
HANSON, William 118
HARDING, John M. 76 82
  Marcena 87
HARDY, Albert P. 57
  George W. 46 Peter 49
HARFORD, Ida L. 79
HARGRAVE, James 28
HARLOW, Lorinda 115
  Nathaniel 128 R. K. 69
HARMON, Edward R. 45
  James O. 37 John 64
  William H. 64
HARPER, Ex-mayor 3
  George T. 105 Hosea T. 45 James 8
HARRINGTON, E. S. 61
  Elijah 58
HARRIS, Elias 45 George Jr. 52 Isaac 44 James 45 President 52 Rose E. 88
HARTFORD, Emma 112
HARTLEY, Capt. 42
HARVEY, Nellie A. 57
  Stephen 69
HASKELL, Micajah 10

HASKELL (continued)
  Sumner 74
HASTIN, Jesse 67
  Joseph 67
HASTY, J. A. 114
HATCH, Eliza J. 54
  James E. 28 Jane B. 79 Roselvena 78
HAWKS, Annie C. 126
  Cyrus 126 Emily 126
HAYDEN, Charles A. 106
HAYES, Mary A. 112
  William 81
HAYNES, Mr. 54
HAZEN, John H. 73
HAZEY, Russel B. 30
HEALD, John 48
HEALEY, Sarah F. 65
HEARD, William 51
HEIDELBERT, Mary A. 56
HEIRLIGHY, Thomas L. 41
HELLINGER, Joseph 27
HENNESSY, John 98
HERBERT, Johanna 118
HERN, John 109
HERRICK, Joshua 128
HERRIMAN, Capt. 105
HERSEY, General 133
HERVEY, Sadie F. 115
HICKEY, 128
HIGGINS, Mary E. 79
  Stephen C. 2 Susan 113
HILL, A. M. 117 Bryant 68 Ella 27 Hattie J. 79 Horatio 98 Laura R. 61 Marshall 108 Mrs. 9 Nancy P. 57 Nettie C. 37
HILLMAN, A. P. 16 Mary 54
HILTON, Ivory 77 Nathan, Jr. 132 135 P. R. 28 George 127
HIMES, William L. 16
HINDS, Elisha 130
HINKLEY, Clara C. 134

Portland Transcript

HISCOCK, Abner S. 23
HOAR, Attorney General 8
HOBART, Bertha 107
HOBBS, Charles H. 54
HOBSON, P. M. 91
HODGDON, Clara 50
HODGE, J. C. 127 Miranda
  E. 127
HODGES, Mary E. 49
HODGMAN, Daniel 117
HODSON, Capt. 2
HOLBROOK, Levi 61
HOLDEN, Charles F. 103
HOLLAND, 76 Joshua 86
  W. S. 10
HOLLEY, Eliza 29
HOLLIS, Enoch 57
HOLMAN, Horace 46
HOLMES, Annie P. 83
  Freeland 62 Martha 5 18
HOLT, 25 Harrison 124
HOOKER, Mr. 35
HORR, Edwin 82
HOUSTIN, Tommy 121
HOUSTON, H. C. 124
  Officer 133
HOWARD House, 75
HOWARD, Charles 6
  Fannie R. 115 Fanny
  75 Jane A. 6 Judge 77
  Micha 103 Rueben 13
HOWE, P. Osborne 127
  Sophia 50
HOWLAND, Charles A. 112
  James H. 69
HOYT, Jane 42 Jennie
  E. 115 Marcia W. 88
HUBBARD, Blake & Co. 104
HUBBARD, Captain 17
  Samuel W. 54
HUBBS, Susie M. 42
HUDSON, ThomasC. 45
HUGHES, Alexander 55
HULL, Robert 118

HUNNEWELL, Hattie W. 49
HUNT, George 49
HUNTER, Benjamin 89
  Robert 41
HUNTINGTON, Eliza E. 57
HUNTLEY, Martha 57
  Urban 74
HUNTON, Lois M. 124
HUPPER, Mr. 116
HURD, E. N. 24
HUSE, Susan F. 118
HUSTON, David 115 E. W.
  61 Eben L. 134 Francis
  M. 28 Olive 115
HUTCHINSON, Persis 109
HYDE, 48
INGALLS, Cyrus 107
  Ezaa E. 9 Priscilla 107
  Richard M. 124
INGERSOLL, Rebecca J. 37
INGRAHAM, Sarah A. 96
IRISH, Joshua B. 82
IRWIN, Fannie E. 82
IVES, C. B. 54
JACKSON, Albert S. 28
  Miss 6
JACOBS, Alvin H. 95
  Joseph 135
JENKINS, 89
JENKS, J. E. 78
JENNINGS, Harnden H. 83
JOHNSON, Alfred 101
  Alvah 65 Capt. 3 Charles J.
  46 Clara J. 115 Ebenezer
  122 Eliza C. 69 Ex-
  president 3 George A. 134
  Jothan S. 69 Louisa A. 42
  Lydia M. 37 President 32
  Seth W. 57 Susan 37
  Theodore H. 49
JONES, Alphonzo C. 99
  Elisha G. 5 Enoch 132
  Lucie 16 Mary T. 126
  Susan 20 Theodora R. 45

JONES (continued)
William 97
JORDAN, 97 A. B. 88 A. M.
62 Barton R. 40 Brisely M.
50 E. S. 112 Fannie 106
Georgia 49 John 106 John
F. 30 Lydia E. 99 Lydia H.
112 Margaret 113 Mary E.
62 Merrill P. 9 16 Mr. 43
Mr. Elder 13 S. J. 49
Susan 99 William 117
William A. 83
JOSE, William H. 62
JUDKINS, Zelotus P. 31
George F. 46
KALER, Mary A. 54
KAPAAKKEA, Ana
Keohokalole 36
KEAZER, Emma 65
KEEFE, 39
KEENE, John 30
KELLEY, John 30 Lizzie
J. 46 Lizzie 4 Robert 19
KELLOGG, Elizabeth G. 130
KELLY, D. D. 105 Seth 104
KELSEY, 32
KEMPTON, Ezra 82
Jeremiah 50 Marshal L. 82
KENDALL, 97
KENNARD, Abby 37
Charles G. 112
KENNEDY, John 50
Sarah M. 50
KENNISTON, Charles 63
KENT, J. D. 128
KETCHUM, W. Q. 10
KEYS, E. R. 16
KIDD, Capt. 13
KIDDER, James 42
KILBORN, A. L. 61 Albert
B. 92 Mary 92 Mary Frost
92 Willie Warren 92
KILBRETH, Joseph A. 52
KILGORE, Abigail 93

KILGORE (continued)
Joseph 113 Lucy 113
P. F. 19
KIMBALL House 99
KIMBALL, Clara E. 27
D. Smith 54 D. H. 117
Emerson 27 Josephine
33 Mary Helen 65
Thomas G. 106
William E. 91
KINCAID, George N. 61
John R. 8 Matilda A. 41
William T. 52
KINGSBURY, William G. 77
KINSMAN, Dr. 108
KITCHEN, John 77
KITTREDGE, Nehemiah 73
KLIPPEL, Christiana 62
Frederick 62
KNAPP, Mary A. 65
KNEELAND, Wilson S. 130
KNIGHT, Abbie Ella 99
David 27 Frank 115
S. K. 107 Storer S. 41
Z. S. 115
KNOWLTON, Charles H. 45
KOINE, Annie 69
LADD, Charley 32
Hiram 18 32 Mary B.
57 Vill 56
LAKE Hill House, 102
LAMB, George A. 113 J. 18
Lorenzo 113 Susan A. 113
LAMPHREY, Freeman 24
LANCASTER House, 36
LAND, Oliver 5
LANDER, Engineer 67
LANE, Ann M. 17 Eva 124
Josiah 17 Lizzie 17 Mr. 56
Rebecca F. 73
LANG, Col. 7 T. S. 3 6
LARRABBE, Benjamin 96
Clara Augusta P. 46
Edward 24 Hannah 96

Portland Transcript

LARRABEE (continued)
  Jonathan 83 Molly 90
  Phebe 83
LAWRENCE, 123 G. W. 80
  James 10 John 121
  Meltiah 111 113
LAWTON, Rose E. 54
LEAVIT, H. Lizzie 41
LEAVITT, Frank J. 103
  Hattie A. 90 Nehemiah
  74 S. R. 90
LEDDY, Eugene 75
LEE, Joseph 37 Nellie 115
LEGROW, Ephraim 37 38
  Jennie M. 134
LEIGHTON, Elvira 56
  Freddie E. 84 Hannah A.
  84 Isaiah 106 J. E. 20
  Oliver H. 84 Remembrance
  68 William 28
LENFEST, Caroline 103
  James 103 William 103
LEVENSALER, Atwood 58
  Joseph 26
LEVERETT, William 99
LEWIS, Annie M. 45 Elijah
  P. 124 George 132 Ida 56
  Jennie O. 103 Rev. Gen. 16
  Wilmot II, 56
LIBBEY, Jennie P. 106
  William M. 106
LIBBY, 90 Abigail 84
  Alberta M. 33 Carrie W.
  113 Charles F. 106 Emma
  135 Frank O. 84 Henry
  H. 84 Hiriam 106
  Joseph F. 14 Lizzie L.
  61 Martha F. 33 Mary 14
  Nellie J. 119 Nora 78
  Rev. Mr. 65 Roscoe 78
  S. O. 31 Samuel 90
  William 61 Woodbury 84
LIDA, Mercy Ann 28
LINCOLN, Abraham 3

LINCOLN (continued)
  Eben 25 James 25
  Sarah 66
LIND, Jenny 8
LINDALL, Charles 84
  Rhoda 84 Rosa 84
LINDSEY, Olive 66
  Stephen D. 129
  William H. 115
LINSEY, Capt. 97
LITCHFIELD, Hannah A. 42
  Henry C. 112 Samuel 126
LITTLE, Edward P. 16
  M. Lizzie 16 William D.
  101
LITTLEFIELD, Almon 100
  Charles 18 Eben 7
LIVINGSTONE, Dr. 98
LOCK, Linnie H. 47
LOCKE, J. C. 94 Linnie
  H. 51 Timothy H. 94
LOCKWOOD, Timothy H. 94
LOGAN, William 108 118
LOMBARD, William H. 46
LONG, Julia N. 79
LONGFELLOW, I. P. 105
LONGLEY, Mr. 48
LOOMER, Maria E. 118
LORD, Brackett T. 122
  Estella L. 115 Mary
  A. F. 115
LUGGEE, Mr. 105
LOUGH, John 132
LOVEJOY, Josephine B. 112
  Maggie A. 49
LOVELL, Sarah T. 50
LOVEWELL, A. B. 99
LOVITT, E. W. 107
LOW, Cephas W. 99
  Marcia E. 73
LOWD, Eliza A. 73
LOWELL, Annie E. 69
LOWRY, John 26
LUCAS, William W. 78

LUCE, Roland 104
LUDWIG, Jacob G. 65
LUNT, Mary Ann 84
  Ruth E. 79
LUGUES, Addie W. 45
LURVER, Samuel 115
LYON, Nathan P. 57
MACARTY, John 108
MACE, Hiram A. 30
MACKIN, Joseph F. 69
MACOMBER, Ellen M. 130
MADDOCKS, 31
MADDOCK, Daniel E. 59
  John F. 59
MAGUIRE, 120
MAINS, Climena 57
MALLENHAM, Addie N. 119
MALLORY, George S. 119
MANCHESTER, Eliza A. 129
MANSFIELD, Bell A. 54
MANSON, Mary 130
MANTER, E. L. 52 Ezra L. 35
MARBLE, Benjamin 109
MARCH, Rhoda M. 83
MARDEN, James 52
MAREAN, Rosilla P. 49
MARK, Charles H. 83
MARRINER, Charles 119
  Rosie F. 122
MARSH, John N. 106
MARSHALL, Cornelius R. 16
  John 117
MARSTON, 14, 19 20
  Lendall C. 96 Nellie M. 10 Phebe E. 110 W. H. 110 Willie E. 110 Wilson 2
MARTIN, George W. 108
  Isaac 105
MASON, Josephine 115
  Laura F. 74 Samuel 16
MASTERMAN, D. W. 27
MATTHEWS, Charles 129

MATTHEWS (continued)
  James E. 37
MAXWELL, Franklin 118
  Martha L. 100
MAY, John W. 73
MAYBERRY, Betsey 100
  James L. 10 Lyman F. 49 70 Richard 100
MAYO, Mary A. 41
MCCARTHY, 118
MCCAUSLAND, A. B. 120
MCCLURE, George 29
MCCLUSKY & Co. 2
MCCOE, George 34
MCCONKY, T. S. 28 U. S. 28
MCCRILLIS, Randall 93
MCCULLY, Daniel 36
MCCURDY, George 19
  Major 102
MCDONALD, Alex 13
  Catherine 60 Hannah 122 Henrietta 115 Thomas 122 Mary R. 10
MCDUFEE, Henry H. 65
MCFARLAND, Capt. 108
MCFARLIN, Robert 58
MCGILVERY, William 29
MCGINLEY, Mr. 48
MCGOWAN, John 88
  Francis A. 28
MCINTIRE, Isreal T. 28
MCKAY, Thomas 10
MCKEEN, Oliver H. 45
MCKENNEY, Aaron 89
  Charles 35 Hillman B. 80 John 89 Verlinda 83 Samuel 89
MCKENY, James 50
MCLAND, Mary 110
MCLAUGHLIN, Henry 133
MCLAUGHTON, Mr. 111
MCLELLAN, Mary F. 16

MCMANUS, Maggie J. 126
MCPHETERS, Esther 73
MCRONALD, Marcia 28
MCVICKER, Miss 44
MEADER, Tobias 76
MEANS, George T. 82
MELVIN, Emma H. 96
MERCHANT, T. J. 55
MERRILL, 25 Benjamin 110
  Eliza 69 Ella S. 69 70
  Ezekiel 113 Henry 110
  Isaac 19 Julia 109 Louville
  H. 112 Luther 123 Mr. 93
  Nellie A. 129 132 Timothy
  69
MERRILL'S, 30
MERTON, John 64
MERSERVE, Emma D. 103
  Esther F. 132 Ezra H. 58
  James G. 132
MILLAY, Joseph 95
MILLER, Deborah E. 47
  Dorcas 54 Eunice 122
  James 3 Margaret 83
  N. J. 6
MILLET, H. M. Maria 73
MILLETT, Alonzo 56
MILLIKEN, Charles 36
  Elias 36 J. A. 97 J. R. 3
  P. S. 97
MINOTT, John W. 127
MITCHELL, H. B. 45 Joseph
  41 L. B. 77 M. W. 30
  Mary B. 34
MODERATION Mills, 59
MOGAN, Michael 98
MONTGOMERY, Celia S. 50
  Robert 116
MODDY, Eugenia A. 99
  George W. 124 Hattie A.
  122 Jennie E. 106
  Samuel 21 William 58
MOON, Emery 43
  Margaret 43

MOOR, C. R. 68
MOORE, Alfred J. 115
  Asa R. 56 Henry 94
  Mrs. 93
MOORES, Ella F. 61
MOORS, Robert 68
MORGAN, Charles H. 33
MORRIETTE, Victor 97
MORRILL, Ex-senator 25
  Jacob 93 Lizzie A. 91
  Lot M. 86 Mr. 44
  Senator 128
MORRILLS, 101
MORRISON, John 10
  Mary W. 45
MORSE, C. W. 49
  Enoch 124 Happy 124
  J. P. 24 Joseph 42
  Prof. 64 Seth 59
MORTON, Robert 122
MOSHER, Edwin 52
  George W. 78
MOULTON, Alphonso 9
  O. T. 9 16 27 (2) 45
MUNROE, J. S. 125
MURPHY, 128 James 49
  Kate 74 Margaret J. 115
  Rev. Father (2) 69
NASH, Julia M. 78
NASON, James H. 65
  Lauraa 57 Mary Ann
  34 Stephen 34
NEALLEY, James, Jr. 69
NEEDHAM, Evi F. 100
  Mary A. 100 Steven H. 100
NEIL, Sarah 113
NELSON, Alfred 59 Henry
  L. 130
NESMITH, Isaac C. 16
NETTLE, Margarette 129
NEVENS, Martha 91
NEWELL, Roscoe G. 128
  Sumner R. 128
NEWHALL, Frank W. 95

Portland Transcript

NEWHALL (continued) 112
NEWTON, Wesley 43
NICHOLS, John 75 Lowell 58
NICKERSON, D. 79 Heman 113
NICKLAS, Theodore 133
NILES, Clara A. 50 Cora W. 57 May Lizzie 57
NOBLE, Emma E. 50
NOIR, Victor 134
NORTH, Charles A. 74 Gertrude R. 74 Media A. 74 Miranda 96
NORTON, Emma A. 121 Micha W. 111
NOWELL, Henry 28
NOYES, Callie 103 Henry D. 103 Jennie D. 57 William S. 73
NUTT, Commodore 48 Laura M. 120
NUTTER, Mr. 114
NYE, Mr. 6 Nathaniel 130 Thomas 31
OAKES, Emma W. 46
OAKFORD, Capt. 112
OBER, Samuel 94
O'BRION, Joseph 62
O'CONNELL, Catherine 112 Margaret 41 Mary 130 Maurice 112
O'HARR, 111
O'LEARY, Hannah 122
OLIVER, 62 Benjamin 39 Wesley 46
ORAN, Mary E. 28
ORMSBY, Carrie 106
OSBORNE, William 54
OTIS, James S. 46 Mary 124
OXFORD House, 55
OXNARD, John T. 123

PACKARD, C. 41 Jerome 123
PACKHARD, L. Annie 16
PAGE, Dexter W. 61 Ira G. 110 Robert 80
PAINE, William 107
PALFREY, Cazneau 101
PALMER, Julia M. 83
PARKER, C. C. 100 C. P. 83 Charles E. 58 Enos 122 George W. 107 Harriet E. 77 78 Phineas 58 Rev. Dr. 98 William 47
PARTRIDGE, Benjamin G. 16 H. 131 L. Maria 79 Mulvy 56 Winfield S. 96
PATCH, Fannie 30 Jesse E. 20
PATRICK, Lucy P. 134
PATTEN, George F. 79 S. 97 Stephen 83
PATTERSON, 26 Polly 46 Emma D. 61
PAYSON, A. M. 10 C. 10 E. P. 13 Emma C. 132 Henry M. 132 Marion 132 Woodbury R. 10
PEABODY, George 64
PENDLETON, William 77
PENFIELD, Harriet N. 99
PENLEY, Ada 104
PENNELL, Albert 84 C. J. 107 Elvira 84
PENNEY, Ephraim 65
PEPPER, Elbridge 119
PERHAM, Kingham 96 Martha H. 96 Sidney 40
PERKINS & Co. 2 George F. 61 Isaac 56 James 20 Joana F. 57 Mary Lizzie 10 11 Nettie L. 78 Sarah A. 10 William M. 7
PERLEY, Col. 117 Willard

Portland Transcript

PERELY (continued) 13
PERRY, Amos 9 J. Frank 121
PETERS, John A. 15 128 Sarah B. 122
PHILIP V, 2
PHILLIPS, Albert O. 96 Lewis 87 88
PICKERING, Alvah S. 115
PIERCE, George 111 Henry W. 46 John 113 William T. 17
PIKE, 95 Capt. 2 F. A. 2 Samuel H. 124
PILLOW, Gideon 112
PILLSBLOW, Frances E. 130
PINKHAM, A. 60 Leander 111
PIPER, David N, 58 Eliza A. 122
PITMAN, William F. 41
PITTS, Benjamin 82
PLAISED, Clara M. 73 E. F. 79 John F. 23 Sarah S. 113
PLUMER, Dr. 26 J. C. 29
PLUMMER, Abba 57 Dana 28 Hiram T. 29 Martha 95
POLLISTER, Mary E. 112 Mr. 12
POLLOCK, Fred A. 134
POMEROY, Mary 57 S. L. 2 Senator 15
POOLE, James 88 91
POOR, Charles B. 33 John A. 15 Sarah E. 49 William C. 50
POPE Pius IX, 8
POPE, John W. 5
PORTER, Rufus 130 William 130 William H. 50

POTTER, Elbridge 72
POWELL, Johnny 77
PRATT, George T. 57 James 69 Officer 108
PRAY, William H. 49
PRENTISS, Julia A. 49
PRINCE, Matilda 115
PRITCHARD, B. F. 78 91 109
PRITHAM, Henrietta A. 122
PROCTOR, Stephen T. 116
PROUTEY, Hiram 116
PURINGTON, E. 37 George A. 10
PURINTON, Nellie L. 33
PUTNAM, George A. 10
QUIMBY, Jeremiah 114 S. S. 48
QUINCY, Frank C. 124 Helen M. W. 110
QUINT, Martha 17 Mary A. 83 Samuel T. 17
RACKLIFF, William B. 48
RADFORD, William 124
RADNOR, Earl 33
RAITT, Jefferson 35
RAND, Albert L. 41 Joel 68 Wilson S. 49
RANDALL, John W. 37
RANEY, William 31
RATTLE Trap Mills, 97
RAYMOND, Henry J. 49 Solomon 32
RECORD, Samuel 115
REDLON, Albert 124 Jane 124 Nathaniel 124
REED, Henry 28 Joseph 24 Margaret 28 Rodman V. 51 Sarah A. 96 Standish B. 65 Stephen W. 134 Webster 102
REEN, Dennis 41
REMICK, Philip W. 57
RENDER, Maggie 100

REUEL, Dr. 112
  Nellie A. 112
REVEL, 114
REYNOLDS, John 24
  Louis 89
RICE, Hattie S. 91
  Mary 91 Sawyer 91
RICH, Charles H. 79
  Esther 46 Ida Louisa
  79 Sophia A. 79
RICHARDS, Emery B. 79
  Henry S. 120 Mary H. 96
  Narcissa S. 126
RICHARDSON, Abbie A. 83
  Celestia H. 114 E. Amanda
  16 Emma H. 45 Frank 121
  Mr. Isaac 60 Mrs. 60 Orin
  26 Thomas 62 William 46
RICKER, Agnes O. 28
  Amanda C. 16 Hattie 115
  James A. 124 William 100
RIDEOUT, Nathaniel 100
  O. B. 42 R. 106
RIDGEWAY, Henry 84 85
RIDLEY, Joseph 115
RIGGS, Sarah D. 42 46
RILEY, Peter 76
RING, Frank W. 13
RIPLEY, Hannah 79 Hosea
  94 John 98
ROACH, Charles W. 135
  Charlie E. 135 Ellen 135
ROBBINS, Benjamin 106
  Capt. 17 Charles H. 47
  Mary 50 Rosilla 50
ROBERTS, Jasper A. 93
  Jasper 90 John H. 121
  Moses S. 121 Rufus 109
  William A. 115
ROBINSON, Betsy 82
  Charles 12 Charles F. 16
  Charles I. W. 37 Edward
  131 132 Elbridge G. 49
  Ellen M. 121 H. Frank 149

ROBINSON (continued)
  Lucy 91 William 74
  William B. 83
ROBY, James 117
ROGERS, Charles 135
  Charles O. 20 63 Hugh
  42 James 104
ROLFE, Emma C. 126
  Margaret 119 Nellie A.
  54
ROLLINS, Amos 90
  Franklin J. 6 Hattie
  L. 112 Helen M. 96
ROOT, Rev. Mr. 106
ROSE, Frank 68
  Margaret B. 16
  Ellia G. 49 Etta A. 9
ROUNDS, Elizabeth 62
  Harriet J. 79
ROWELL, Charles H. 2
  P. 37 39
ROYALS River
  Manufacturing Co. 59
RUGG, Clara 110
RUMERY, Abigail S. 135
RUSSELL, Dora B. 45
  Ephraim 115 Laura J. 88
  S. Chapin 83 William 55
RUST, Frank 82
SAMPSON, Julia 27
SANBORN, 72 Edwin G.
  121 Elizabeth 88
  George 88 Josie H. 88
  Ruel 98 William H. 56
SANDERSON, Roscoe 45
SANDS, John W. 96
SANFORD, Mary A. 126
  Thomas S. 126
SARGENT, Clara J. 28
  Eleanor W. 10 Ellen J. 112
  H. R. 10 Oscar W. 46
  Stephen 71 Walter 133
  William H. 10
SAUNDERS, Harriet 41

SAUNDERS
 Helen A. 79 John 82
SAVAGE, David 86
SAWTELLE, Charles 93
SAWYER, 59 Abbie 113
 Clara J. 134 D. J. 105
 E. M. 105 J. W. 100 106
 Jane B. 41 52 John J. 131
 Mark H. 34 S. B. 132
 Stillman 115 T. W. 49
SCAMMON, Ambrose 25
SCHELLENGER, Wealthy
 57
SCOTT, 98 Andrew 37
 Annie F. 91 Capt. 66
 George 5 Henry W. 37
 James 35 John A. 87 91
 Walter 15 William 113
SCRIBENER, Mary 134
SCRIBNER, Mary 132
SEARLS, Daniel C. 57
SEAVERS, G. W. 101
SEAVEY, Evelyn C. 57
 Gardiner E. 126 John F.
 116
SEIDERS, Annie L. 49
SENTER, Mary A. 33
SEWALL, Narcissa 46
 Samuel 46
SEYMOUR, Ex-Governor
 54
SHANNON, Victor 64
SHAPLEIGH, Eunice 88
SHARP, Elizabeth 45
SHATTUCK, Mary F. 124
SHAW, Alpheus 66 Brother 1
 Cornelius 75 Hettie L. 122
 Jacob 52 Serena 2
 William M. 17
SHEA, Jeremiah 32
 Michael 32
SHEHAN, John J. 41
SHELDEN, Charles 112
SHERBURNE, Emma 51

SHERMAN, Adrianna F. 115
 Fred M. 115 Gen. 67
SHERWIN, James P. 126
SHIBBLLES, James E. 65
SHINN, George W. 56
SHORT, Georgie 56
 Joseph H. 90
SIBLEY, R. 74 S. A. 37
SILSBY, Oliver E. 16
SIMMONS, 58 Bridget
 75 Sarah 130
SIMMS, 120
SIMONTON, Putnam 130
SIMPSON, Bishop 8
 Thomas 108 William
 R. 91
SIMPTON, Jane N. 129
SINCLAIR, Mr. 55
SKILLIN, W. 122
SKILLING, James S. J. 27
SKILLINGS, Almira 127
SKOLFIELD, Rose 79
SLATER, Sarah 1
SLEEPER, Mr. 39
 Willie 44
SLEIGHT, William R. Jr.
 119
SMALL, Benjamin 134
 Benjamin L. 122 George
 E. 43 George Edwin 42
 Gilbert 134 Isaac 134
 John C. 82 Mr. 14
 Susan 46 William B.
 124
SMALLEY, 125 George
 80
SMART, Col. 30 Mary F.
 37 Nicholas E. 46
SMILEY, James 113
SMITH, Adriana M. 54
 Calvin 52 Clara E. 79
 Cynthia P. 49 Daniel 90
 David F. 99 Frank B. 78
 Fred J. J. 37 H. Paris 132

SMITH (continued)
   Hattie A. 50 Howard D. 78
   James E. 114 132 John R.
   25 L. 34 Lydia Howland
   119 M. Augusta 106 Mary
   57 Mary E. 109 Mary G. 56
   Mary T. 74 Peter C. 108
   Samuel E. 57 William S. 31
   Zemna R. 51
SMOUSE, George 94
SNELL, Eleazer 56
SNOW, Cyrus S. 74
   Elizabeth 46 J. C. 129 124
   Josiah B. 130 William 74
SOMERBY, Abiel 42
SOULE & Co. 31 A. J. 10
   Charles 41 Eunice A. 78
   Ida J. 10 Jonathan 50
   Pierce 10 15 Sarah F. 10
SOUTH Dover Mill, 14
SOUTHWORTH, Rev. Mr. 69
   87 109
SPEAR, Job 58
SPRAGUE, Jesse G. 39
   Mercy 135 Mr. 44 45
   Senator 9 William H. 30
SPRINGER, Samuel 23
SPROWL, Joanna V. 49
   Mary E. 37
STACEY, Uranus 33
STACKPOLE, George 112
STAHL, Oliver E. 41
STANFORD, Cynthia 126
STANLEY, Ephraim 86
   Frances 79 Jacob 58
   Rufus 86
STANTON, Ex-secretary 15
STAPLES, Carroll 74
   Charles H. 17 Edward F.
   34 Freeland A. 33 George
   D. 99 Gertie Maud 17
   Harlow P. 78 Henrietta 17
   James S. 45 Susie 65
   William C. 33

STARBIRD, Lafayette 56
STEELE, Mary Ann 112
STERLING, Johiah 11
   Philena 11
STETSON, Amasa 46
   "Father" 14 Gerry
   & Co. 80 William P.
   14
STEVENS, Ann D. 51
   Charles A. 43 E. A. 24
   George H. B. 112 J. 7
   Jacob 42 John L. 6
   Nathaniel 131 132
   Oliver 100 Oliver P.
   96 Thomas C. 96
STEWARD, Andie M. 73
   I. D. 100
STICKNEY, Paul 29
STILPHEN, Augustus M. 99
STOCKBRIDGE, Anna 127
   John 127 Napoleon B. 73
STONE, A. Mabel 66
   Charles F. 115 David G.
   57 John 69 Lydia F. 121
STORAB, Augusta M. 79
STORER, William A. 49
STOVER, Benjamin W. 27
   Lettie 78
STOW, Harriet Beecher 73
STRATTON, Charles H. 49
STRICKLAND'S Ferry, 30
STRONG, E. C. 83 Isabel
   W. 28 Jane W. 100 John
   E. 28 Sarah E. 28
STROUT, J. A. 27 Joshua F.
   13 William E. 45
STUART, Charles M. 37
   Robert 15
STUBBS, Joseph W. 33
   Reuben 34
STUDLEY, John 113
STURDIVANT, Louisa 29
STURGIS, B. F. 124
   Nellie E. 95

Portland Transcript

SUMNER, Sarah 130
Senator 27
SUNDERLAND, Rev. Dr. 33
SUTHERLAND, Mary A. 10
SWAN, Zachary T. 88
SWASEY, Harriet M. 10
Horatio J. 10
SWEET, E. C. 6 Elvin C. 56
SWEETER & Merrill 112
SWETT, Lizzie P. 122 Sarah T. 48 Stephen 115
SYMS, Ida E. 46
TARBOX, James 29
TASKER, B. F. 28
TAYLOR, Elish B. 28 Joshua L. 124 Mary 49 Nancy 113 126 Robert 117 Sarah F. 47
TEASDALE, Isadora F. 27
TEMPLETON, Mary A. 29
TERRILL, Jacob 101
TEWKSBURY, Charlotte N. 4 5 G. A. 99 George 69 124 George A. 103 106 Jacob 4
THAYER, (Whitman) Deborah L. 33
THOMAS, Annie 96 Annie E. 28 Betsey 122 C. D. 96 E. A. 96 General 27 James W., Jr. 130 Katie E. 126 Nellie F. 54
THOMPSON, 109 A. P. 106 George A. 103 Greenfield 59 J. O. 73 James E. 47 Margaret Ann 111 S. H. 109 William 106
THORN, Susan A. 91
THORNE, John A. 96 Susan T. 96 W. H. 96
THORP, Lewis 49
THRASHER, Mrs. 67
THURLOW, E. W. 65
THURSTON, George W. 37
THWING, E. P. 112
TIBBETS, June C. 57

TIBBETS (continued) William 93
TILTON, Gen. 108
TITCOMB, Beniah 79
TOBEY, Miss 60 Sarah 37
TOBIE, Betsey 101 Richard 103
TODD, Henry F. 10
TOLMAN, John S. 114
TOM Thumb, 108
TOOTHAKER, Capt. 29 Franklin B. 78 Terris A. 134
TOPPING, Mercy 88
TOTMAN, Joseph 108 Rachel 113
TOWN, George 118
TOWNE, Daniel J. 91 Edwin 50 H. C. 27
TOWNSEND, Daniel R. 110
TRACEY, S. Maria 29
TRACY, Oliver 131
TRAFTON, John H. 96
TRASK, Lydia 45
TREAT, Eva Maria 56
TREFTHEN, John M. 50
TRICKERY, Henry Sargent 69
TRIP, Bessie a. 58
TRIPP, L. A. 132 Silas 41
TROLLOPE, 48
TRUE, Augustus 59 Augustusa W. 66 Harriet 66 Herman A. 66 Lena Florence 37 Samuel 50 Susan C. 109 W. H. 18
TRUMBULL, Jonathan 54
TUCKER, Payson 24 Rosetta D. 49
TUELL, Ebenezer 6
TUERO, C. T. 103
TUFTS, William 50

TUKEY, Carrie S. 49
TURNER, Addie 65 Capt. (2)
  32 Clementine 115 Flora
  65 Horatio G. 65 Hiram
  103 John 65 Samuel E.
  73
TWITCHELL, 9 George 3
  Mrs. 9 21
TWONEY, Hugh 98
TYLER, Alexander 51
  Gertrude H. 51 Julia P.
  51 Lizzie 132 Mary E. 79
URAN, James W. 60
VAIL. H. M. 122
VAN COOT, Widow 20
VAN HORN, Annie I. 124
VARNERY, T. M. 101
VARNEY'S Mills, 34
VAUGHAN, Hester 33
VERRILL, W. H. H. 88
  Isaac 114 Widow 67
VINING, James 89
WADE, Eugene H. 41
WADLEIGH, Elisha 115
  Mary J. 115
WAGNER, William 104
WAITE, Jennie M. 46
  Stephen 115
WAKEMAN, Alonzo 93
WALBRIDGE, 123
WALDEN, Sarah A. 27
WALDRON, Georgia M. 46
WALKER, Dr. 86 Edmund L.
  28 Emery O. 33 John 95
  Nathan 12
WALLACE, Edward 52
  Elizabeth S. 45
WALLS, Ann M. 50
WALTON, B. F. 30
WARD, 89 Artemus 14
  John 126
WARDWELL, H. B.122
WARE, John, Jr. 72
WARREN, Etta J. 34

WARREN (continued)
  George 102 103 J. C. 42
  Martha 28 Minnie 48
  Mrs. 63 Vienna H. 115
  William 25
WATERS, Granville 61
  Helen 49
WATERHOUSE, Abbie 46
  Alexander 10 Lemyra C. 46
  Mr. 15 Nancy 28 Walter
  S. 109
WATERMAN, Georgia A. 78
WATKINS, Cassie M. 106
  Eli P. 106 Sarah L. 106
WATSON, W. H. E. 109
  Marcus 30 Mary E. 88
  Oscar F. 30
WATTS, John 80
  Margaret F. 46 S. &
  Co. 80
WAY, George 134
WEBB, County Attorney
  77 78 D. C. 27 Francis
  E. 102
WEBBER, Climena 110
  George H. 10 Joseph F.
  49 Marietta C. 10
WEBSTER, Harriet N. 82
  John 78 Joseph 82
WEEKS, George H. 45
  Martha E. 121
WELCH, Abbie M. 121
  Alex 93 Nancy A. 57
  Patrick 118
WELD, Caroline 62
WELDEN, Nathaniel 132
WELLS, CHARLES 42 96
WENTWORTH, Lydia F. 49
WESCOTT, Emily Francis
  132 R. T. 107 William
  115
WESSER, Count 7
WEST, Isaac 47
WESTCOTT, Charles 133

WESTCOTT (continued)
J. P. 134
WESTON, Benjamin 86
Carrie A. 61 James 115
WESTWOOD, James W. 106
WETHERBEE, Calvin S. 46
WHARTON, Charles 40
WHEELER, Mary L. 88
WHITCOMB, Calvin 42
WHITE, 76 Annie 28
David, Jr. 24 Horace W.
73 Jasper 96 Joseph 88
Mary S. 96 Thomas G. 96
William 28
WHITEHOUSE, George C.
69 Sarah L. 78 William P.
56
WHITMAN, Mary C. 78
Sarah J. 78 W. E. S. 109
WHITMARSH, Hattie W. 61
WHITMORE, 133 C. W. 20
John C. 132
WHITNEY, Herman S. (2) 78
Keziah 113 Robert 75
WHITTEMORE, Capt. 71
WHITTEN, Eliza B. 99 H.
Imogen 73 Jennie S. 99
Nettie W. 46
WHITTING, 66
WHITTLE, Mary Olive 79
WIGGIN, 44 Hattie B. 73
WIGHT, Almon 49
Eliphalet 84
WILKINSON, Western E. 16
WILLARD, John 124 Sarah
B. 124
WILLEY, M. R. 81
WILLIAMS, 90 Delia 103
Freeman 13 Hanna H. 112
Henry 94 Nancy L. 99
Robinson 95 William 97
WILLIS, Thomas Leonard 88
William 124
WILLOUGHBY, L. C. 28

WILSON, Annie 61 Charles
H. 76 Frederic A. 61
Sibbel 69
WING, Elsie H. 99
Patrick 81
WINSLOW, Emma F. 96
Ethelyn 96 Hiram H. 1
Jason H. 96 John F. 50
Martha S. 78 Mary 113
Mrs. 77 Sarah E. 49
WINTER, Orren 73
WIRZ, 126
WISWALL, L. 115
WISWELL, J. M. & Co. 74
Luther 49
WITHEE, Mr. 14
WITHINTON, Charles H. 61
WOOD, Alice 132 Henry L.
58 Mary 37 Mary E. 95
Walter J. 45
WOODBURY, Daniel 126
Frank P. 88 William W. 61
WOODMAN, E. W. 6
Franklin 119 Harriet
69 Jabez 91 M. 12
WOODS, F. 54 Henry J. 46
WOODWARD, Conductor 67
George H. 57
WOOL, Gen. 90
WORMELL, 52 C. M. 133
E. S. 16
WORTHING, Samuel H. 107
WRIGHT, A. F. 112 Annie
E. 50 Ellen M. 112
Madison 133 Sarah M. 73
WYLIES, Jennie L. 69
WYMAN, Charles 112
Dellie 89 Mary E. 112
Sarah 89 W. 12
Augustine 89
YATES, Martha 88
YEATON, Hannah 40
YORK, Henrietta 63
YOUNG, Brigham 53 63

Portland Transcript

YOUNG (continued)
  Charles 74 David 23
  George M. 83 Harriet J.
  74 John 32 Malvina J. 56
  Susan 88

*About the Author*

Elaine Morrison Fitch has had a strong curiosity related to her ancestral background all her life. After fits and starts of gathering information she began seriously devoting time to it after her father's death in 1993. She soon discovered that her ancestors on her father's side had settled Lubec, Maine and been notably active in the Revolutionary War. The Morrison side has been more of a mystery but she has successfully traced them back to Rathlin Island, County Antrim, Ireland.

Elaine's efforts in compiling newspaper abstracts evolved out of purchasing a complete year's volume of the 1848 Boston Cultivator at an antique auction. The painstaking transcription of entertaining stories of events, stories, marriages and deaths has been a labor of love for her. The subsequent relationship with Heritage Books has resulted in an ongoing series of nineteenth-century newspapers being brought back to life in a form that is designed to assist researchers in finding lost relatives, provide history buffs with interesting accounts of events and give an overview of life in America at the given time. Each volume is carefully indexed with a Full Name Index in order to provide the reader with easy access to information.

Elaine continues to work on additional manuscripts for publication. She and her husband live in a log cabin in New Hampshire.

www.ingramcontent.com/pod-product-compliance
Lightning Source LLC
Chambersburg PA
CBHW060821190426
43197CB00038B/2178